How to Start Your Own Cleaning Company

Go From Start-up to Payday in One Week

By Angela Brown

For information about this title or to order other books or electronic media, contact the publisher:

Life Long Publishing
PO Box 49266
Charlotte NC 28277

Printed in the United States of America

To contact the author:
Facebook: https://www.Facebook.com/SavvyCleaner
Twitter: https://www.Twitter.com/SavvyCleaner or @SavvyCleaner
Pinterest: https://www.Pinterest.com/SavvyCleaner
Linkedin: https://www.linkedin.com/in/savvycleaner
Email: AngelaBrown@SavvyCleaner.com

Introduction

Hi. If you're here because you have an interest in house cleaning or in upgrading your life by starting your own house cleaning company. Welcome.

There an irresistible force that draws entrepreneurs into the residential house cleaning business – either a startup you created or a franchise you purchased. If you're here it's because you recognize the escalating 49 billion dollar a year residential cleaning services industry* as a way to supplement your current income, or you just want more control of your schedule as you pay your bills.
(* The US Commercial and Residential Cleaning Services Industry, compiled by Market data Enterprises, Inc.)

House cleaning is an industry that is nearly recession proof – when times get hard, people work more to pay the bills, they are home even less to clean, and they outsource their cleaning – which means more business for you and me.

Another reason that house cleaning is an awesome business model is this: unlike a regular 9 to 5 job if you get fired, you're not out of business. You simply add another customer into that available time slot and keep going. And I'm going to show you how do such an awesome job that you will never get fired, and your clients will never want you to leave.

Franchise or start your own?

So should you buy into an existing franchise like Molly Maids, Merry Maids, The Cleaning Authority, or Maid Brigade? Or should you start your own house cleaning company from scratch? There are pros and cons to both.

If you are not sure of the differences, I've created a comparison chart you can download free. http://savvycleaner.com/franchise

For the sake of this book we are going to assume you are going to start your own house cleaning company from the ground up.

Preface

Hi there, I'm Angela Brown Oberer – I go by Angela Brown (Brown is my maiden name) for my house cleaning company because Angela Brown is an easy name to remember – and if people remember your name, and can pronounce it easily, they can refer you to their friends. It's an easy name for their friends to remember as well.

I started house cleaning back in 1991 – I was living in Charlotte, North Carolina working a few part time jobs. (Delivering newspapers for the Charlotte Observer and waiting tables in the evenings at Harpers Restaurant.) One of the waiters at Harpers cleaned houses during the day and talked me into coming to work with her.

I didn't know much about house cleaning – I was the kid growing up who slighted my chores and always tried to get out of helping around the house. LOL. *You probably know or have a kid like that am I right?*

On my first day of cleaning houses I got fired – not for being slothful, but for asking too many questions. "Why are we sweeping junk under the rug instead of moving the rug and sweeping under it?"

The next day, I started my own house cleaning company. I had no idea what I was doing but my business philosophy is: provide a great service that people need at a fair price and do it consistently.

I asked a lot of questions from my clients. I wanted to meet and exceed their expectations. What was it going to take for them to feel like they had the cleanest home on the planet? I did endless surveys with my clients and you know what? They gave me honest answers and lots of feedback. *I'll admit some of it was hard to take,* because *I was the business.* I was the one responsible for making the corrections. I took it really personally, and used the suggestions to empower me.

Then I created a fail-proof system that is super easy to duplicate and works consistently on ALL of my clients. I incorporated what was important at one house - to all my houses. And then a mysterious thing happened.

My house cleaning business exploded!

Suddenly I had more referrals than available time slots. I had a waiting list with thirty people...

My house cleaning business blasted into a full-fledged operation becoming my only job and I was working on weekends.
I hired several house cleaners to help me.
Hiring more people seemed like a simple solution to my rapidly growing database of referrals.

It was far from simple.

My clients had become family. I wanted to protect my family. I didn't want just anybody to show up and clean. I wanted to make sure the new housecleaners were drug screened, background checked and had been trained properly to clean. I was sending new house cleaners into my client's homes, (*a home is usually a person's most valuable asset*) and they were working around my client's families, children, pets and parents. This is not something I took lightly.

The training process was extensive and attrition was high. Not to mention the expense of bonding, insurance, workman's comp, cleaning supplies and vehicle expenses for my employees. Eventually I spun each house cleaner into their own business with a full roster of clients, and scaled back.

Oh my gosh, house cleaning is a scalable business. It is so totally cool! You can add new clients or cut back according to the different demands life throws at you. I cut back, working only enough to pay my bills, and returned to school to take some business, marketing, and management courses, all the while implementing my new found skills to my house cleaning company.

Over the next 24 years my life was a tidal wave of house cleaning success, while I surfed with the ebb and flow of life. I moved to various cities, each time relocating my house cleaning company and starting over from scratch.

My easy-to-implement tried and proven system had me up and running with a full pack of new clients within two weeks of each move. This is not guesswork – it is a proven system and it's simple.

I got married, bought a house, helped raise relatives children, sold our house, bought another house and pursued an acting career. All the while house cleaning part time or full time. It was the one constant thing in my revolving world and the referrals flooded in.

I kept training new house cleaners and rolling them into their own house cleaning companies with a full database of clients (It was a way to serve my clients who had faith in me and sent endless referrals my way.) And then it hit me – I should train Independent house cleaners. There is no official training, and no consistency in the work we provide – and it would allow me to streamline my training process.

In the fall of 2015 I had so many referrals, I was giving away 40-50 house cleaning referrals a month, for several months, to any house cleaner or maid service that had any sort of business savvy and any open time slots.
I interviewed and screened dozens of independent house cleaners and then I overloaded them with referrals until they told me to stop sending business their way. Imagine that.

That's when I wrote this book:

How to Start Your Own House Cleaning Company: & work from referrals only
http://www.HowToStartYourOwnHouseCleaningCompany.com

Then came the demand for a house cleaning blog where people could write in and ask specific questions about their house cleaning businesses and where customers could ask why their house cleaners did things a certain way.
http://www.AskaHouseCleaner.com

The system I use flat out works. It's been test marketed inadvertently for 24 years with the people I've trained who are still thriving in business after all these years. Some of them running multi-million dollar house cleaning franchises, while others are working solo, providing for their families on a part time basis. Bottom line, it works and it can work for you too.

If you're not sure if you have what it takes to start your own house cleaning company, check out this free
http://savvycleaner.com/do-you-have-what-it-takes

Foreword

Written by Julie Brown
House Cleaning and Organizing Specialist

What you're about to read here is:

1. Easy to apply
2. Proven to work
3. Gets results fast

I have been cleaning professionally for over 20 years. I wish there had been a book like Angela's when I got started. This is a thorough, step-by-step guide to all the business details you need to know to take your own company from 0 to successful in no time flat. It's an easy to understand explanation of the mechanics of house cleaning. Read every word here and do everything this book says. It answers all the questions you have. So, pay attention.

You will experience major changes in your business and personal life. I say personal life because when your business is running like a well-oiled machine, it frees you up to spend time on the things and people you love.

You're going to get some amazing tools here, and instructions on how to use them. This guide will produce a turning point in your life.

Angela and I are sisters and have both spent most of our adult lives in the house cleaning 'business'. We were raised in a large family and work skills were taught and implemented from an early age. Angela has combined everything we've learned and practiced over the years in this fun, illustrated, simple formula to walk you through the business aspect of starting your own house cleaning company and becoming your own boss! What's better than that?

Angela and I have exchanged experiences and strategies over the years to discover new and better ways to serve our clients. Angela goes beyond ordinary measures to problem solve and create efficient methods to save you time and your customer's money. You're on the threshold of perhaps the greatest opportunity of your life. These tools catapulted me out of an excellent life, into an extraordinary life I love. You are holding in your hands a way to make that happen for yourself. Its works!

You have waited your whole life for this. Go out and take your moment. This is your year! The world needs what you have.

-Julie Brown

All the Things We Are Going to Cover Here

- ✓ How to set up your Home Office
- ✓ What Office Supplies you are going to need
- ✓ Your Company Logo
- ✓ Choosing a Company Name
- ✓ Your Uniform
- ✓ Creating Your Company Image & Brand
- ✓ Setting Your Rules & Policies
- ✓ How to Choose a Territory
- ✓ Everything You Need to Know about Creating Flyers
- ✓ What is a Worksheet and Why You Need One
- ✓ How to Bid Jobs
- ✓ What to Charge
- ✓ What kind of Car you need
- ✓ Punctuality
- ✓ Confidence Builders
- ✓ How to Build Instant Credentials
- ✓ Bonding & Insurance
- ✓ Mulligans
- ✓ How to Get an Endless Stream of Referrals
- ✓ Referral Fees – How Much Should You Pay?
- ✓ Billing and Collections
- ✓ Payments

What We Are NOT Going to Cover:

(*All of the following "must know" courses are bundled together in the Fast Track Training at www.SavvyCleaner.com

- ➢ Business Ownership Best Practices
- ➢ Best Health Tips, Tricks & Hacks to have unlimited Energy through the Day
- ➢ Ways to Avoid Pet Allergies and Sickness from Client's homes
- ➢ Rules for Lunch and Smoking Breaks
- ➢ Best Marketing Strategies for Ongoing Success
- ➢ Recommended Green Detergents to Use on Each Type of Surface
- ➢ How to pick out the best Vacuum, Mop and Step Ladder
- ➢ Best Customer Service Practices
- ➢ Client Privilege – how it can make or break your business
- ➢ Working Around Pets, Kids & Elderly People
- ➢ Poison Control
- ➢ Fire Safety
- ➢ OSHA Rules & Regulations
- ➢ Calling in Sick
- ➢ Travel & Vacation Time
- ➢ What to do When Things Go Wrong
- ➢ Troubleshooting for Success

- Dealing with High Maintenance Clients and when and how to fire them.
- Law Suits
- Theft Accusations
- Disagreements with Clients
- Damage Control
- Emotional Distress
- Sexual Harassment
- Tips, Tricks and Time Saving House Cleaning Hacks
- On-going Training and Network Support
- How to Clean a House from Top to Bottom (Incudes: Toilets, Dishes, Stairs & Railings, Trash & Recycling, Desks, Bookshelves, Carpet & Stains, Hardwood Floors, Lamps, Shades and Chandeliers, Mirrors, Glass, Bathtubs, Showers, Computer & TV screens, Weight, Gym Equipment, Pool Tables, Arcade Games, Knick-Knacks & Trinkets, Stainless Steel, Granite, Travertine, Onyx, Brass, Copper, Tin, Tile, Vinyl flooring, China cabinets, Playrooms, Toy boxes, closets, garages, attics, drawers, cupboards, bathroom vanities, Range tops, Microwaves, Kitchen Sinks, Wood Furniture, Wicker Furniture, Wrought Iron Furniture, Suede Furniture, Leather Furniture, Window Screens, Silk Plants, Laundry, Bath mats & Rugs, Beds & Linens, Bakers Racks and End Tables, Dining rooms & nooks, Doors, Windows and so much more.)

➢ Miscellaneous How-to
   (Incudes: Moving packing, unpacking, Holiday
   Parties, Birthday Parties, Holiday Decorations,
   removing nail polish from furniture, removing water
   marks from furniture, defrosting freezers, Oven
   cleaning, Coffee Stains, Wine Stain remover, general
   cleaning, removing paint splatters and drips,
   Ironing, Table settings, Spice racks, pantry
   organization, and so much more.)

Satisfied customers are talking:

"Have you ever thought of cloning yourself? If you could teach other house cleaners to be just like you...you would be rich." They just don't make 'em like you anymore."

- Kyle Curtis

"I grew up with a house cleaner, and have had a house cleaner ever since owning my first home, but we've never had a better house cleaner, affordable, reliable, consistent, charming and professional than Angela Brown. I hope she never quits. She is awesome."

— Stacey Matros

"I just love to be wowed, and I just was when I hired Angela Brown to come clean my house. She arrived exactly when she said she would be here, was totally professional, worked like mad, and then made me cry because my house was so beautiful. WOW and WOW!"

— Jenny Sanders

"Just had to take a moment and let everyone know what a GREAT job Angela Brown does at house cleaning! If you need your house cleaned one time, or repeatedly she is THE person to call! Excellent rates and Excellent work! Call her at (Angela's phone included) and tell her Hans Newton from Nextdoor referred you!"

- Hans Newton

"You made me want to live in my house again."

– Cheryl Eckert

"A lady one street over is going to call you, she was complaining about how lazy her house cleaner is and I just couldn't stop bragging about you. Of course I had to give her your information, I hope you're still taking new clients. You always do such a great job...all of the time."

– Mari Price

"I tell people about you every chance I get. You do great work and it's so nice to come home to such a clean house. My family just loves you."

– Mary Thompson

How to Set Up Your Home Office

What type of office set up do I need?

The best thing about starting your home based house cleaning business is that you can be up and running in a few minutes with the right equipment – some or all of it you may already have.

So you don't need a fancy office, and you certainly don't need to rent space for an office or to store your supplies. You can work right out of a nook in your home with a computer (laptop or desktop), internet connection and a printer.

What type of calendar should I use?

You will need a calendar app on your smart phone, so you have it with you at all times for scheduling.

CalenMob (http://www.appxy.com/calenmob/) or Google Calendar (https://calendar.google.com/calendar/) will do the trick. It will happen a lot that you will be with a client and they will decide to reschedule, or book an additional cleaning -- and you will want to grab your phone, check your schedule, and then book your next appointment right then and there with the client present.

Avoid the "let me check my schedule and I'll get back to you" routine because you don't want to get home and then have more follow up work to do. And if you are like me, you will get home and be distracted by other pressing matters and forget to get back to your client, and that is not professional.

Train yourself to schedule and confirm appointments as you go – then boom, you're done.

How will I be using the internet for my cleaning business?

Your internet connection will allow you to do all of your online learning for your house cleaning company and also attend troubleshooting and marketing webinars, and participate in the Savvy Cleaning Network which is peer-to-peer help and ongoing support. You will also use it to search Google for odd requests that clients will ask like: "How to clean between the layers of glass in an oven door." Not common knowledge but when you show up having an answer – it means big tips for you.

 If you don't have the resources for a computer today, and you are unable to download PDF files, and don't have good internet access – visit a local public library. With a library card (free in most US cities) you can use their computers with internet access. Use the public libraries computers until you earn enough money to buy your own computer and internet service and printer.

What will I be printing?

You will need a printer so you can print up your flyers and your worksheets, both of which are your two biggest marketing tools and you will use your printer every day.

Other than that, we're going to keep it really simple for now, and just include a shelf in your laundry room or bathroom for all of your cleaning supplies. Preferably your shelf will be next to a sink where you will mix supplies and solutions and refill empty bottles.

You can pick up a durable, galvanized steel shelf that won't rust at Home Depot or Lowes for $25-$50. They assemble easily in a few minutes with included instructions. I got a small one 12 inches deep, 24 inches wide and 60 inches tall. Fits in a very small space and holds about a month worth of supplies.

We will go in to greater details later on what supplies and solutions to carry. For now, all you need to focus on getting is a shelf to keep all your supplies organized.

Office Supplies You Will Need

Flyers

There are several inexpensive and almost free ways we will be marketing, but today or tomorrow, when you don't have any business yet, we will be running flyers to announce your new business. For these flyers you will need a ream (500 sheets) of colored paper. Pick a color, any light color will work. If the paper is too dark, you will not be able to read what you've printed.

You can buy this at OfficeMax, Office Depot or Staples. Reams of colored paper range from $10 to $15

For your start up flyer we'll print two flyers per page and this will save paper and printing costs.

If you are good at cleaning, and you work the referral system you will only be running flyers once. So this is a fixed one time cost.

If you have a printer, inkjet or laser, make sure the paper you buy is compatible with the printer. Usually something like the paper shown will work in either, but ask a store assistant if you're not sure.

If you are buying a new printer – choose a laser, it will keep the ink from bleeding on a printed page if the page gets wet.

Stapler

You will be stapling your worksheets so I recommend buying (if you don't already have one) a stapler. It doesn't have to be fancy, it just has to staple.

Pens

You'll need a pack of cheap Bic pens. You will carry one of these with you to every house to fill out your worksheets. You can usually get a pack of ten pens for a buck or so. And you will lose them, they will go through the wash in your pockets, so don't spend a lot of money on pens, just use cheap pens.

Sortkwik

You will want to use some type of finger moistener for running flyers. More on this in the "Flyers" section. But pick some up while you are at the office store today so you don't have to make another trip to the store tomorrow.

Paper Cutter (Optional) or Scissors

If you already own a paper cutter you'll use it to cut your flyers in half. (You'll be printing 2 flyers per page.) If you don't have a paper cutter, you can borrow one from a friend or your church, or you can use scissors. Paper cutters range from $15 to $300 so don't go crazy and buy one just for your one time flyer creation. It does make the job easier – but it's optional.

Computer & Printer

If you do not own a computer or printer -- check out BestBuy, Amazon, Staples, OfficeMax or Office Depot. You can get a really great late model laptop for $249 or less, and a really great black and white laser printer for $100 or less.

Worksheets

Work sheets are multi-purpose, and are the life-blood of your marketing efforts.

1. With the worksheet you will close your original sale with a client.
2. You will use your worksheets as a progress report to prove the work you have done to a client. (This validates your satisfaction guarantee.)
3. It is your invoice
4. Your receipt
5. And your biggest referral tool.

This is an ongoing expense and for this I recommend using plain white paper.

To get started, you will need a ream of 500 sheets of white paper (20lb paper, bright white is good) sold individually for $3 to $6 and you can buy paper anywhere. Walmart, Costco, Target, Office Depot, OfficeMax, Staples etc.

You can buy a case of white paper between $20 - $40 and save money. A case usually includes 10 reams of paper.

It is assumed that you have a computer, and a printer, and if you do, all of the office supplies you need to start your own house cleaning business should be under $20. These are purchases you will make the first day of your business. That's it!

(If you have to buy a computer, printer, office supplies and a case of paper, you're looking at $400 or less for enough supplies to open your own house cleaning business. And you will be using these for the remainder of your business.)

Save your receipt from any purchases made for office supplies, shelves, computers etc. Now that you are starting a business, you will tax deduct all of these purchases on your annual income filing.

If you are really shoe-stringing it – borrow a computer and printer from family or friend, until week two when you have money coming in and can buy your own.

In a pinch, you can download a sample of the worksheets and flyers. Simply change the information and logo and have them printed for about $.10 per sheet (x 2 flyers per page = $.05 per flyer) at OfficeMax or Staples until you get a printer. You will need computer and printer for the long term so get one as soon as you can afford one if you don't already have one. Here is an office supplies checklist

http://savvycleaner.com/office-supplies

Choosing Your Company Logo

Do I need a logo?

Do you need a logo to start your own house cleaning company? No. It's optional, but I highly recommend getting or creating one. A logo for a house cleaning company would be a fun little picture that says what you do. It might be a man with a vacuum, or a woman with a broom, or a house with a smiley face on it, or something of that nature.

You can begin right away and start cleaning houses – but having a logo will make you look more like a real company. All real companies have a logo. It is part of their branding. If you have a logo, you will use it on your flyers, on your worksheets, you can use it on custom embroidered shirts you have made as part of your company uniform, for car magnets, your website and so on. In other words, on ALL OF YOUR MARKETING. (None of these are mandatory to start cleaning today though. Just something to think about.)

What's so great about having a logo?

Check it out. When you see golden arches you know what company it represents. Am I right? I don't even have to say the company name. You know immediately it means fast hamburgers, fries, happy meals, and a drive through, with coffee, breakfast, ice cream cones, and apple pie. It is because they have done a phenomenal job with their marketing. World-wide the golden arches tell a story everybody recognizes. And how about the Starbucks logo. Can you picture it in your mind? Sure you can. Even without the word Starbucks attached, when you see the green circle with the lady in the middle, you know its coffee, and free Wi-Fi. Logos do that for you. They tell your story in one glance. So at some point you may want to create a logo that says what you do, and you'll want to use it on all of your marketing. It's part of your brand.

Having a logo adds immediate credibility. So if you are starting from scratch, and you don't have house cleaning experience, having a logo will make it look instantly like you are a real company, and you know what you are doing. Once you find a logo that works for you, keep it. Don't keep changing it every few months.

How do I get a logo?

If you want a logo – you can hire a designer to create one, (this usually costs $500-$1,000) but there are several services that provide high quality logos that you can buy for a lot less money (from a simple online kit) and start using today. Check out http://www.freelogoservices.com/ where you can type in the information for your business and then choose from their selections of logos. You can tweak them and customize them to your needs. Only when you are satisfied with your choice do you pay for your logo. Starting for as low as $35 and the prices go up from there.

Or you can create a contest at
http://www.99designs.com/ where you pay $199 to host a
contest where designers from all over the globe compete
to create a design that suits your needs. (If you pay more,
more designers will join the competition), then you choose
your favorite. Boom, you're done. Your $199 or however
much you chose to pay, pays for the logo.

Google the words: (Logo design) and explore all of the
online options for house cleaning logos -- and find one that
suits your likes, needs and budget. Some out of the box
logos even let you register and trademark your logo and
company name. (Again not mandatory, just optional.

We found our Savvy Cleaner logo (a blue and green tear
drop in the shape of a house, with a little door at the
bottom and sparkles coming from the windows) at
http://www.freelogoservices.com/ It was affordable,
allowable to register and trademark for this program --
and it says what we do. (We make houses sparkle -- and I
chose the drop shape and colors to unconsciously suggest
environmentally friendly).

When I first started cleaning houses twenty years ago, I
didn't have the money for a logo, and I didn't have any
graphic design skills, so I combined some fun pictures of
two generic people, one with a broom and the other
hugging a house, a small valentine was coming out of the
house. It was a cheesy logo and the pictures suggested
"we love our house clean."

Having a logo is entirely up to you, but it's something to think about as you get started.

Naming Your Company

What name you use for your business is entirely up to you – but comes down to how your business is structured and how you intend to pay your taxes.

Your company name is part of your brand and as you grow your business you may want to add a company name to your marketing efforts. This is NOT something you have to do today.

This will become necessary as you create a web page and do advertising (if you ever need to – this program will show you how to simply run flyers for two weeks and then work off referrals for the rest of your career. So advertising is a non-issue for now.)

As a small start-up – one man or woman show, it is advisable to use your personal name.

This way when you are paid, the money will go in to your personal or small business checking account and you will file your personal taxes either single or jointly with your partner/spouse.

This keeps the taxes part super simple because you are not registering a company name, and then paying yourself as an employee, and then paying a self-employment tax.

You can add a company name to your worksheets and your flyers if you want. My company name is Life Long. It is on my flyers and my worksheets but I've never had a Life Long website, or car magnets, or phone book advertising, Angie's List www.angieslist.com advertising, or Yelp www.yelp.com or Yext https://www.yext.com/ pages advertising for my house cleaning business.

I'm Angela Brown Oberer – I go by Angela Brown (Brown is my maiden name) for my house cleaning company because Angela Brown is an easy name to remember – and if people remember your name, and can pronounce it easily, they can refer you to their friends. It's an easy name for their friends to remember as well.

Do you have a name that is easy to remember?

Think of this scenario: Megan and Ken who are neighbors, are standing at a school bus stop waiting for their kids, and they start talking about their day. Ken, a stay-at-home Dad has been cleaning his house all day and is pooped. He really needs a house cleaner to help out. Megan, a savvy woman who works from home has a house cleaner she highly recommends, but doesn't have the house cleaner's contact information with her.

"You should call my house cleaner, her name is Angela Oberer."

While Megan remembers the difficult name, Ken does not. Not sure he heard it correctly, Obgur? Oberay? Oburrer? Ober? Obrer? Oberger?

...and the referral never goes through.

Instead Megan says: "You should call my house cleaner, her name is Angela Brown, or Jenny Jones, or Tom Sparks."

So much easier to remember, and refer. Also if she refers the company "You should call my house cleaner she has a company called Life Long Cleaning" Ken gets home and can't remember if it is Long Life, Life Long, Longer Life something like that... and as he googles it finds a different company and hires them instead."

So the object is to make it super easy for people to find you, and refer you.

Suppose Megan, brings with her the next afternoon to the bus stop, a worksheet I left behind. On the worksheet, Ken sees all of the things I do while cleaning a house, AND my contact information is at the top and presto. Ken can call me too.

Who are you?

Do you have a name that is easy to pronounce and easy to remember? If not, choose one to use for your business. You can even make up a name if you like – just make sure that whatever name you choose, you add that name to your personal bank account so when checks are written to you using that name, they are cashable. The form you will use at your bank is a simple DBA (Doing Business As) form.

For twenty years on my bank account I had name Angela Brown listed. When I got married fourteen years ago I added, Angela Brown Oberer and Angela Oberer to the account. Any check written to those names will be cleared in my account.

I also have those same combinations of names registered on my PayPal account with two separate email accounts *Angela@AngelaOberer.com* and *Angela@AngelaBrown.com* as emails you can send money to. Try sending some money there, you can see how it works, it's easy.

Should You Wear a Uniform?

Do I need a uniform?

Yes you do. And here's why: When you show up looking the exact same way every time you show up, you send an unconscious message that you are offering a consistent product or service. If you show up one day with sweat pants and your hair in a ponytail, and then next time in jeans and hair down, and then next time in sweats and a bun – nobody knows quite what to expect. (Even if they are just watching you on a home security camera.) Each time there will be an unconscious jarring where they will have to figure out what is going on. Keep it super simple. Wear a uniform that is appropriate to the job they are expecting you to do.

When you go to the ER and a guy walks in with a lab coat, you immediately feel like he knows what he is doing right? He must be a doctor, he has a lab coat on. But if he tried to take your blood and he was wearing jeans and a biker Tee shirt, you might think twice about handing your veins over. A uniform, like a picture, speaks a thousand words. It also builds confidence which is really important if you are just starting your business. You want to "look" like you know what you are doing right from the start.

Your uniform doesn't have to be expensive or have embroidered logos or a company name on it, although those are options. I recommend saving embroidered logos until you are ready to hire someone else and expand your business and then you will want to dress like twins wearing matching uniforms etc. Right now, you are one person and your object is to get up and running right away with minimal start-up costs.

So my suggestion is buy plain simple clothes at a department store or online at a uniform store, but buy several (six or seven) of the same outfits so you have clothes to wear every day and you're only doing laundry only once a week.

Shirts

For your uniform shirt you can pick any color you want. I suggest a solid blue, solid teal or a solid green, it suggests cool colors and environmentally friendly. These few colors are easy on the eyes, and go well with most any skin tone, even if you have pasty washed out skin like me.

 A shirt with a collar is preferred as it suggests an upper class clientele and it looks really professional. We see the golf community wearing collared shirts, and want to blend in with that community rather than shouting "blue collar worker" by wearing an old ratty tee shirt. You want to project the image of a private boutique company servicing an exclusive upper class clientele. The shirts do not need to be monogrammed or embroidered or have any fancy printing on them. Save your money for now.

You want to pick a shirt that fits you well, that you can tuck in. Don't worry if you are carrying a few extra pounds, if your shirt is tucked in while you are working, you will still be presenting a well pulled together image.

I buy my brightly colored collar shirts at Costco for $14.99 each and I buy seven of the same color each spring. (This year they happen to be blue Tommy Hilfiger and have a small TH logo) This gives me one to wear every day for five days, (five shirts) and two new ones to toss into the mix halfway through the year when the others get soiled or stained.

If you can't find what you are looking for at a wholesale club like Sam's, Costco, check Kohl's. They have inexpensive golf or polo shirts that you can find seven of the same shirt in your size.

At the end of the year, I rotate all the shirts and this year's work shirts become next year's gardening shirts I wear when I mow my yard or clean my own house etc.

Wearing the same outfit every day takes the guesswork out of what you will wear, so it saves time getting dressed each day.

Pants

For uniform pants, I buy Dickies from an online uniform company they come in camel, navy and black.

http://www.workwearusa.com/dickies-workwear/dickies-pants/ ($9 - $29 a pair)

Navy and black are preferable since they don't show grime as easily, as lighter colored pants. Uniform work pants from a uniform company are very durable and they don't fade in the wash allowing them to be worn for three to four years of daily use without needing to be replaced. I've had the uniform pants I'm wearing now going on three years and they'll hold out for another year or two and still look great.

They are also made of some magical type of fabric that doesn't require ironing. So I can take them straight from the dryer, hang them up and they are ready to wear.

The dark pants go well with solid color shirts and they have big cargo pockets on the side where you can hide your cell phone. There is also a back pocket on both butt cheeks that are buttoned. This is perfect for stuffing the handle of a Swiffer duster in the back pocket without it falling out – this way you always have it within reach when you need it.

Pick one color of shirt and one color of pants and stick with that combo. Remember we're going for consistency here. If you keep changing the color of clothes, it's subtle, it has absolutely nothing to do with the quality of work you do, but your clients know something is not the same as before, and they will assume it's your work. Solve that question before it becomes conscious.

Shoes

For shoes, I wear comfortable tennis shoes with good support and I do not remove the shoes when I go into homes. Rather I buy in bulk from a medical store, http://bit.ly/1X8490y shoe booties or shoe covers that slide right over my shoes. This protects my shoes from scuffing hardwood floors as I clean.

Gloves

And from the same medical supply company (usually Saraglove.com or who ever is cheaper when I'm ready to buy again) I buy nitrile gloves http://bit.ly/1TFO1pm (you can also buy latex or plastic) but I find non-powdered nitrile gloves are more durable than plastic or latex. They are all about the same price and come in a box of 100 for an average of $9.99 per box. (You can also buy latex gloves in a box of 100 in the automotive department at big box stores and in the medical or pharmacy section of places like Costco and Sam's.)

Hair

If you are a guy, cut your hair short and shave. Unless you are an actor and you have a signature look, a tidy clean professional look sends the branding message that your service is also well groomed.

If you have long hair as a girl or guy, when you get out of the shower in the morning (and yes, you do shower before going to work, even if you will need a shower when you get home), make sure when your hair is wet, to pull it back in a tight knot. (Bun, clip or hair tie.) This removes the need for styling before you go which will again save time on your morning routine.

I have shoulder length hair and I add a glob of conditioner to my towel dried but still wet hair, work it through my hair, (which acts like moisturizing gel to hold the hair in place), then do a side sweep of wet hair over my forehead and back into a tight bun with a clip. Four bobby pins hold wisps from getting away, and it's very tight, clean, look that promotes consistency, and it keeps my hair from falling in the Clients house – which I will later have to clean up.

Order your uniform shirts, pants, shoe covers and gloves in the first few days of starting your business. While you are running flyers and setting appointments, your uniforms can be shipped and in transit.

Your uniform costs with shoe booties and gloves will be about $300 per year. This is an annual, recurring cost, and is tax deductible, so save your receipts.

Your Company Image

Image is a broad range of how people perceive you in the market place – and thank goodness for marketing 101 we can direct other people's opinions of us and show them what to think about us through the image we project.

Now you've probably just read the section about uniforms, and if you haven't, please go back and review it before you land here because we will be building on that personal image branding.

Your image is a display of your beliefs. Here's how it works: you have seven seconds to "show" someone what you are all about as a business and a business owner.

In seven seconds clients will decide if they want to work with you or not. Do you believe in cleanliness and order? How you show up and what you leave behind will be an extension of your beliefs. And they all fit into your personal brand.

Your professional image

So let me ask you this: if you arrive to clean a house in an old beat up car with muddy windows, and a bumper that is taped on with duct tape – what is the first impression the client will have of you?

True or not, they are going to assume you are careless. (I.e. you got in an accident and are cheap. You didn't bother to get your bumper fixed. You don't care about cleanliness since there is mud on your windows, and if your car is full of wrappers, junk and lose cleaning supplies, that you're just disorganized and a total mess.)

Immediately their mind goes to a place that asks: "if they don't care about their own personal belongings, why should I trust them with my most valuable personal asset – my home? And you haven't even gotten out of your car yet.

How you show up is your professional image. You have 100% control over that.

You don't have to have a fancy car, but it should be in working order and it should be clean.

If you are selling a cleaning service - your car should ALWAYS be clean. Especially because it will be sitting in front of your clients house for several hours on cleaning day.

I recommend joining an unlimited car wash plan at a local car wash company like Autobell http://www.autobell.com/ or SamsXpress http://samsxpresscarwash.com/ that for $25-$30 a month. You can drive through as many times as you like and get your car cleaned. I have one I use, and I end up washing my car three to four times a week. My car is always clean and I am methodically projecting the clean tidy image that is consistent with my brand.

Professional Image is your car, your cleaning supplies and your company.

The good news is you will not be having clients over to your storefront – because you don't have a storefront, so you don't have to worry about what your home office looks like. You do however need to pay attention to how you arrive.

When you arrive, are your supplies in a neat caddy, clean, full and ready for the job? Or are you sifting through mounds of junk in your car for a can of cleanser that rolled under the seat?

Believe it or not, home security cameras can pick you up -- and clients can zoom in and watch you and your arrival process. Trust me, they will do this.

Get out of your car, take out your cleaning supplies in one swift and organized movement, lock your car door and approach the house.

Do it like you are an actor on the big screen, and you've rehearsed this scene hundreds of times. The cameras are rolling and all of the neighbors are watching you from their windows to see if this is the person they want to hire for their next cleaning project.

I promise you this – the neighbors will talk about you – good or bad. Direct them to a positive conversation by the image you project.

Personal Image

Personal image is how you show up, and when you are on the job. This is you.

Your overall appearance, your uniform, your shoe covers, your hand gloves, etc. When your clients recommend you, this is the image they have showing up at their friends' homes. They don't want you to make a fool of them. The referred you because of the work you do and the image they have of you and your company, and they want you to show up exactly the same way.

Company Image

Your company image is what you leave behind. If you are running flyers, the very first impression your new prospects will have is the flyer you left behind. It is one reason if you choose a logo, it must be cohesive with the products or services you are selling. If you have a paint brush as your logo connected to some small flowers, and you are selling house cleaning services – it doesn't make sense. People will be confused -- and something as simple as the wrong logo will keep people from hiring you. People respond to emotion before they respond to logic. And if you've made the emotional and the logical perceptions to hire you incomplete – bam, you're not going to get any business.

Can you describe your business in way that excites people to hire you?

If you are just starting your house cleaning business and you can't imagine what your company image looks like, it's going to be hard to sell. If you can't imagine it, how on earth are you going to explain it to somebody who calls you on the phone? Get a really clear picture in your mind what your business looks like, how you work, what clients can expect when they hire you. Practice explaining it so it rolls seamlessly off your tongue. Make it easy – super easy to repeat the image you've created about you and your business, so your clients can share that image easily and promote you with referrals.

Be punctual

Showing up on time to bid a job and when you actually show up to do the job itself is paramount. If you show up exactly at the time a client expects you, then you have reinforced the idea that you are reliable. Unfortunately, if you show up late, you have reinforced that image as well.

Referral image

Your worksheets are your progress report. They are your biggest marketing piece that you will ever leave behind. Your worksheets need to be organized, tidy, current, etc. They are your invoice, and your receipt. Your worksheets have your rules and policies on them and it has your contact information. These worksheets will become your best advertisements as clients hand these out to their friends along with their personal word of mouth referral.

Make sure you don't forget to bring customer worksheets each time you clean a house. Make sure you carry them with you on a clip board so the papers aren't wrinkled and wet from cleaning supplies. And make sure that you have enough printer in the ink cartridges in your printer so it doesn't look like a ghost skipping off the page, rather than the text you are intending to print. Your image, personally and professionally will set you apart from all of the other house cleaners they've ever had.

Remember you are not just a house cleaner...you are the company owner.

Your Rules and Regulations

What are your policies?

You are the boss now. You get to decide what the rules for your business are.

What hours are you open for business?

Are you closed on holidays or do you charge more to work a holiday?

Do you accept credit cards for your business or cash only? You get to decide.

The key is to have an answer for all of the following questions. There are no right or wrong answers, but you need to decide in advance how your small business operates, so when the phone starts ringing with people who need a house cleaner, you know how what to say.

This is an activity for today. Write the answers down to these following questions. If you run flyers today or tomorrow – the phone is going to start ringing and these are the questions they are going to ask. How you answer them will determine if you get the job. Really spend some time on this section.

If you stumble, and you're not sure of your policies, people won't take you seriously. They will think you have never been in business and you have no idea what you're doing.

People don't want to hire house cleaners who have no idea what they are doing.

Think about the following questions and come up with some answers that work for you.

1. Do you work by the hour?
2. Do you work by the job?
3. Do you only do house cleaning?
4. Do you set up for parties or clean up after parties?
5. Do you do moving (moving in or moving out) cleans?
6. Do you charge more money or the same money for a moving clean?
7. Do you do random cleanings or do you *only* have weekly and bi weekly clients?
8. If my regular cleaning falls on a holiday will you be working?
9. Do you charge more to work on holidays?
10. What hours do you work?
11. Do you work weekends?
12. How long have you been in business?
13. Is there any special training you've gone through to learn how to house clean?
14. Are you OSHA trained and certified?
15. Have you ever been fired from a house and why?
16. Do you have references?
17. Do you do laundry?
18. Do you do dishes or empty the dishwasher?

19. Do you do pet sitting on the side?
20. Is it okay if my pets hang out in the same room as you cleaning?
21. Is it okay if my kids are in the same room as you cleaning?
22. Are you bonded and insured?
23. Are you licensed to house clean?
24. Do you clean windows?
25. Do you only clean houses or do you also clean offices?
26. Do you detail cars?
27. Do you defrost freezers or clean out the fridge?
28. What type of cleaning chemicals do you use on hardwood floors?
29. Do you have your own vacuum?
30. Do you bring your own cleaning supplies?
31. Do you do miscellaneous projects?
32. If I refer my friend, do I get a referral fee or discounted cleaning?
33. Am I supposed to tip you for your service?
34. Do you clean out the hot tub?
35. What happens if you get sick?
36. Do you cancel or reschedule on me or do you just show up sick?
37. Do you charge a rescheduling fee if I have something come up and have to cancel?
38. Am I supposed to give you a key so you can get in my house or do you need an alarm code? Or both?

39. How do you protect my privacy with that key or code?
40. Do you have a safe place to keep a key or a code?
41. Do I need to be home when you come to clean or can I be at work?
42. Are you the person that is coming to clean my house?
43. Is it just you cleaning or are you bringing a team of people with you?
44. Are the people you bring with you bonded and insured?
45. What is your screening policy for people you hire?
46. Do you do background checks or drug checks on the people you bring with you?
47. Can I do a background and a drug check on you?
48. How do you prefer to be contacted? Email, phone or text?
49. What happens if you break something while you are at my house?
50. Are you going to tell my neighbors about me, my home, my habits and how messy my house is?
51. Do you set times to come back so I know when you are coming or is it random?
52. Do you always come the same time on the same day?
53. Do you show up on time?
54. Do you clean the same stuff each time or do you rotate chores through the house?

55. Do you use environmentally free chemicals?
56. How do you know what type of chemicals to use on different surfaces? How did you learn?
57. Do I pay you under the table or do you pay taxes? I'd like to take house cleaning as a deductible expense for my home based business.
58. I work from the house, will it bother you if I'm home the whole time?
59. If I'm working from home, are you going to chat the whole time or will you allow me to get my work done?
60. Do you accept credit cards?
61. Do you offer a guarantee on your work?
62. If I forget to leave you a check, do you still do the work and let me pay you later or do you skip the cleaning?
63. Do you water indoor plants?

There are more questions but these are the most commonly asked. Having answers to these questions will guide you set some rules and regulations and will help you create some necessary boundaries for your business. You need to know the answers, and rehearse them so that when a prospective client calls about house cleaning, you are confident and know how your business operates.

If you decide to create a website, you can answer these questions on your "FAQ" page and it will let prospective clients know how you operate so you don't play 60 questions when you arrive to bid a job.

Everyone will answer these questions differently. How I answer them, based on twenty four years in the business is a separate training class with follow along handouts. As an active member of the Savvy Cleaner Network you will be eligible to attend these trainings and have access to on-going learning.

Consider joining the Savvy Cleaner Network if you are not already a member. Ongoing training and support is crucial to the success of your business.

The cost to join is pennies a day, compared to the training franchises offer. And being a member adds instant credibility to your new business. More info on this can be found at www.SavvyCleaner.com

Choosing a Territory

The good news is that as independent house cleaners we don't have "territories."

Lots of house cleaning franchises tout the fact that they have "protected territories." But all they are protected from is their own franchisees marketing the same brand working in that area. They have no control of competing franchises or independent house cleaners. So go work where you want.

The good news is there is enough business for all of us. I only work in two neighborhoods and there are a dozen different cleaning services in those two neighborhoods. When I get referrals that I can't work due to the fact that I'm working at full capacity and have a waiting list of 30 people, I pass those referrals along to other house cleaners who work in those neighborhoods.

My thinking is since they are already there working, they can save some commute time by picking up the clients I can't help. It doesn't cost me anything to pass along the referrals, and it helps the clients who were referred to me.

#WorkSmartNotHard

Pick one or two neighborhoods that are close to where you live. In this business we don't get paid for travel time, fuel or wear and tear on your car. So don't spend lots of time stuck in traffic, or time commuting, or time lost driving between houses, it's just not profitable.

I work in my own neighborhood and the neighborhood next door. My commute is one to three minutes. That's it.

Pick neighborhoods to work in, rather than single houses along a stretch of rural highway. Neighborhoods have social media sites or closed neighborhood Facebook groups and apps like "NEXTDOOR" http://www.nextdoor.com or "MyNeighborhood" http://www.myneighborhood.com that allow neighbors to talk to each other, recommending house cleaners and other service providers. A good deal of your business will come from these social media sites and neighbors who chat with each other while out walking their dogs, or waiting at the school bus stop for their kids.

Neighborhoods also have the value of peer pressure. You've heard the term "keeping up with the Jones's?" I have clients that have immaculate homes and don't need a house cleaner because they stay at home all day cleaning themselves — but if the neighbors have a house cleaner, they've got to have one too so they can share in the stories and neighborhood banter. It's awesome to be the recipient of this type of peer pressure.

How to Pick a Neighborhood
Pick neighborhoods that are new (0 to 15 years old). Within the last fifteen years home builders started adding

more windows to homes, which means less furniture against windows. The trend is bigger open spaces which means less walls, which means less pictures and knick-knacks hanging on those walls to dust.

Most people with gobs of windows will hire a window cleaner a couple of times a year, so other than the occasional smudge from children or pet prints, windows usually won't be included in regular "house cleaning". Do clarify expectations with clients though when you're hired, so there are no surprises on either side.

A sign from the outside of a newer home, is the newer homes have window panes planted between double panes of glass.

Rather than older windows that have the panes on the outside of the glass, and will quite literally fall apart when you try to clean the corners of each section, not to mention it takes fifteen times longer to clean the old windows vs. the new. Because you have to individually clean each section of old windows, rather than use a squeegee for the newer ones.

Stack the deck in your favor by choosing your neighborhoods wisely.

Even though you may not be cleaning windows – this is an illustration of how the age of property takes a toll. Older homes have lots of "wear, age and structure" problems to consider.

Older homes have split wainscoting, moldings, cornices, and edgings around doors and windows which allows bugs to creep in, which means more cobwebs, spider nests, silverfish, cockroaches, and snails. Once a home is infested – you have to really clean under every cabinet, inside and under every ledge of furniture, every stair, window sill or casement vs. just dusting.

Newer homes have been sealed better.

If you work a full schedule you'll be cleaning 20-30 houses period. Then your schedule will be completely full, so choose 20 to 30 newer homes, rather than the older homes to make your life easier.

Don't discount apartments and condos and follow the 0-15 year rule when choosing as well.

Lots of my clients live in apartments and you can clean the whole apartment from top to bottom in two hours with a really thorough cleaning. Easy peasy.

Geographic Location as Main Hub

If you live in a neighborhood that supports it – work in your own neighborhood. There's something powerful about living in a nice home and being able advertise that fact.

"Hi, I'm Angela Brown, I live in your neighborhood, and I know what we neighbors are looking for in a house cleaning service. I know how long it takes to clean these

types of homes, and I treat all of the homes I clean with the same respect I show my own home." = Powerful

My neighbors know where I live. They drive by, they see my yard and the way I care for my own home – it is a great advertisement.

What you didn't say is: Since we are neighbors I can't be a scam artist, because you know where to find me.

Work hours that fit into your schedule

Lilly, another house cleaner in my area has an evening job as a tutor at a nearby school. She cleans a house in my neighborhood every day before her tutoring job. This way she makes one round trip, avoids rush hour traffic in the morning and evening. She works her cleaning business for four hours a day, drives one mile to her second job where she works another 4 hours as s tutor, and then goes home. One trip consolidated and streamlined. Brilliant!

If you are a busy parent and you have to drop your kid off at school – pick a nearby neighborhood and clean your houses there. That will allow you to work during school, pick up your kid from school, and you've made one round trip out and back for the day. Booyah!

Clean houses near a school

Schools are conveniently positioned between active neighborhoods with busy working parents, teachers, music instructors, sports coaches, doctors, dentists, bankers, realtors, and other independently owned business professionals, all of which are crunched for time and could use some house cleaning help.

School neighborhoods are also good because there are bus stops. At bus stops there are kids -- and parents waiting for their kids. Every day, five days a week morning and afternoon, they chat and they gossip, and they brag. You will be talked about (good or bad) at the bus stop. Think of it as FREE marketing. Woohoo!

Clean houses in a retirement community

Other really profitable hubs include one story pinwheel or ranch homes designed as "active adult communities" or retirement communities. These are often filled with wealthy retired people who want to enjoy their golden years entertaining (not cleaning), or elderly people who are physically unable to do household chores. They also include affluent single adults who don't have kids and don't want to mess with day-to-day tasks like landscaping or house cleaning. You can work non-stop in a community like this and have all the business you will ever be able to handle as an independent house cleaner.

Partner with home builders for last look cleaning's

Some savvy house cleaners have partnered with home builders who toss them all of the final home clean up before the buyers close on the property. This can work to your advantage as builders usually build one community at a time, so all of your business will be in a single neighborhood until they build a new one.

Work with Realtors for move in-move out business

Another profitable hub, and my least favorite, is working with a team of realtors who have a constant stream of move in/move out clients for you. This is a much more random approach to cleaning since the realtors work with anyone who calls them. You have no control over where the move in and outs may come from and it could mean travel up to 30 miles in any direction. If you choose to do this, specify upfront where and how far you are willing to travel. And clarify who is paying you.

I personally don't like working with realtors for the fact that the business (while it may be a steady stream of clients) is not the same client each week. It's not consistent work. You might work three days one week and seven the next. And the hours can be quite random as well. And you have to keep reinventing yourself as each move in/move out client has different expectations. There are often the questions of who is paying you? The buyer? The seller or the realtor?

A house cleaner in our network did an entire move out cleaning only to find that the realtor thought the seller was paying for cleaning, and the seller thought the buyer was paying for the move out cleaning. The buyer didn't know about the cleaning at all – and everybody refused to pay. The house cleaner after trying for three months to chase the money, gave up and ate the cleaning as a loss.

How far should I travel between houses?

As little as possible.

If you have to commute to a neighborhood - make sure that your start and end times for your house cleaning don't conflict with rush hour traffic. Nothing will waste your time and kill your profits faster than sitting in traffic for an hour each way.

And if you are cleaning more than one house in a day, make sure it's in the same neighborhood so you don't waste time driving between jobs.

Maximize your travel time

There are literally hundreds of thousands of podcasts you can download free of charge on iTunes http://www.apple.com/itunes or Stitcher https://www.stitcher.com that cover all areas of interest. Motivate yourself, educate yourself, and entertain yourself during your drive time.

This is your life, and if you're spending part of it in your car – make it count for something.

Here's a list of podcasts I listen to while traveling. Upbeat, motivational, humorous and educational.

http://savvycleaner.com/angela-browns-podcast-list

Should You Run Flyers?

The secret to running flyers

Yes. If you follow this program exactly, you can go from no clients to being fully booked within a few weeks and then work from referrals after that. I've moved several times over the years, and each time we've relocated, I've started my business over from scratch. No clients, same business, new neighborhood, new clientele.

I have used the exact same system, the same flyers, and the same process -- and have received the exact same successful results. So I'm sharing it with you because it works. You are in business for yourself, so you can do whatever you want, and change the system however you want —my feelings won't be hurt. But if you don't have all the business you want — come back to this program and follow it step-by-step and rebuild your business so you have recurring clients and a steady stream of cash flow.

I buy one ream of colored paper. (500 sheets) at Office Depot, OfficeMax or Staples. The cost for this is $10 to $15 dollars — usually like $11.49 or something weird like that.

Use your home printer to print up the flyers and print them in black and white ink. Don't spend lavish amounts of money on glossy brochures or four color printing. You don't want to give the image that you are a franchise with an $80,000 investment who needs to recoup those costs.

You are a one man/woman show out of the shoot. You are professional, but you keep your costs low because every dollar you save, is a dollar in your pocket. Your flyer will tell your customer exactly what type of business you are – and that translates into the client asking "is this the right cleaning service for me?"

So you want to answer questions they are going to ask right on your flyer.

So, what should your flyer say?

The good news is you can say whatever you want it to say. You can have pictures or bullet points.

I've used the same house cleaning flyer for 24 years and still use it to this day because it works. Click on the link and I'll send you a free copy that you can edit - simply change the name, email address and phone number and start using today.

Yes! Send me a Copy I can edit and use today. http://savvycleaner.com/flyers

Or, you can create your own from scratch. Google the term (House Cleaning Flyer). Hundreds of samples of house cleaning flyers will pop up. Some are colored, some are black and white. Some have tear tags, while others appear to be business cards.

Some work and some don't. But Google the term and look at what others have done.

If you're not particular, use mine. It's proven and it works and it will save you all afternoon going down a rabbit hole of graphic design and ad copy.

Flyer do's and don'ts

I do NOT recommend a flyer with tear tags – (Tear tags have a dozen tags at the bottom with just a phone number, and people leave the flyer hanging but tear off a tag,) and I don't recommend leaving flyers on public bulletin boards, telephone poles, bus stops, school bulletins, grocery stores etc. The reason is that people who gather at those places are from different geographical locations. You are going to target your market to one or two neighborhoods so that you are not traveling all over the place. You don't get paid for travel and you don't want to waste time and gas money driving to the next client.

Regardless of what you write on your flyer, you need to answer some basic questions:

- Who are you?
- What are you selling?
- Why do I need your Service?
- How do I get in touch with you?
- Do you have a website or email?
- Do you guarantee your work?
- How much do you charge? Or Are you affordable?

- Are you bonded and insured? *(If you are not, and you choose not to be, do not advertise this on your flyer. Only list it if you ARE bonded and insured.)*
- Do you accept credit cards?
- Do you work weekends? *(If you do not work weekends, do not advertise this either. Only list it if you are willing to work weekends.)*

I print two flyers per page and cut the page in half.

A cut up flyer (1/2 page of an 8 x 11 sheet of paper) fits nicely in a shoebox on the passenger seat of the car for easy access while delivering flyers. A small jar of SortKwik finger moistener can be purchased at an office supply store for about $2.50 and will keep your fingers moist while you keep reaching for the next flyer.

Depending on the neighborhood, there are better times of the day and week to run flyers. What works best for the cleaners in our network is to go around 9:00am on a weekday. We use a weekday because people check their mail on weekdays. Everybody has left for work and you can get in and deliver your flyers before the mail truck comes. Also avoid garbage pick-up day. You don't want to be navigating in and around garbage cans out on the street.

Start on the left side of the street drive slowly down the street with your blinkers (hazard lights) on, and leave your flyer in the newspaper box. DO NOT LEAVE YOUR FLYERS

IN THE MAILBOX. The mailbox is federal property and is illegal to open anyone else's mailbox. If you are caught leaving things in people's mail boxes without paid postage, you can be charged full postage prices for each piece of mail discovered along with a hefty USPS fine. *(And they will find you because your email and your phone number is on the flyer.)*

Instead leave the flyers in the newspaper tubes, or taped to the newspaper tube. Don't be obnoxious with it – you don't want to send the wrong message right off the bat, you just want your flyer to be seen and you don't want to be charged a fine for doing it incorrectly.

Watch for and yield to: cars pulling out of their driveways, kids on bicycles, women or men walking pets etc. Always give them the right of way.

If you see someone out in their yard or if they are at the mailbox when you approach, smile, wave and leave them a flyer in their box. You want to portray your best image even when out running flyers.

You might even consider wearing your house cleaning uniform, in case somebody asks you on the spot to come in and "bid the job". This has happened to me more than once.

You are an advertisement – make sure when running flyers, that your car is clean.

This is a House Cleaning Worksheet

House Cleaning from Life Long... *So you can enjoy the most important things in life.*
Angela Brown / 555-555-5555 / Angela@AngelaBrown.com

KITCHEN
- ❑ Clean Kitchen counters
- ❑ Clean stove tops
- ❑ Clean microwave oven
- ❑ All cupboard and appliance surfaces cleaned
- ❑ Polish furniture
- ❑ Dust baseboards, pictures, lampshades, knick-knacks, windowsills, furniture, light fixtures and other décor.
- ❑ Garbage removal
- ❑ Sweep and mop or vacuum floors

FORMAL ROOM
- ❑ General straightening up
- ❑ Sweep and mop or vacuum floors
- ❑ Dust baseboards, pictures, lampshades, knick-knacks, windowsills, furniture, light fixtures and other décor.
- ❑ Spot clean walls and windows to remove fingerprints and smudges
- ❑ Garbage removal

DINING ROOM
- ❑ General clean up
- ❑ All cupboard and appliance surfaces cleaned
- ❑ Polish furniture
- ❑ Dust baseboards, pictures, lampshades, knick-knacks, windowsills, furniture, light fixtures and other décor.
- ❑ Spot clean walls and windows to remove fingerprints and smudges
- ❑ Garbage removal
- ❑ Sweep and mop or vacuum floors

FAMILY ROOM
- ❑ General straightening up
- ❑ Sweep and mop or vacuum floors
- ❑ Dust baseboards, pictures, lampshades, knick-knacks, windowsills, furniture, light fixtures and other décor.
- ❑ Spot clean walls and windows to remove fingerprints and smudges
- ❑ Garbage removal

Mark's office OFFICE / STUDY
- ❑ General straightening up
- ❑ Complete vacuuming in all carpeted areas
- ❑ Dust baseboards, pictures, lampshades, knick-knacks, windowsills, furniture, light fixtures and other décor.
- ❑ Polish furniture
- ❑ Garbage removal

BATHROOM
- ❑ Sanitation of showers and bathtubs
- ❑ Sanitation of sinks and vanities
- ❑ Mirrors cleaned
- ❑ Floors vacuumed or mopped
- ❑ Toilets cleaned
- ❑ Garbage removal

MASTER BEDROOM
- ❑ General straightening up
- ❑ Dust baseboards, pictures, lampshades, knick-knacks,
- ❑ Beds made and linen changed (if linens are left on bed)
- ❑ Complete vacuuming in all carpeted areas
- ❑ Garbage removal

MASTER BATHROOM
- ❑ Sanitation of showers and bathtubs
- ❑ Sanitation of sinks and vanities
- ❑ Mirrors cleaned
- ❑ Floors vacuumed or mopped
- ❑ Toilets cleaned
- ❑ Garbage removal

OUR NEXT SCHEDULED VISIT:

Wed March 13 @ 8:00am

Whisper is Cat
Melancholy is Dog
Cheryl is live in Grandma

The Magic of Worksheets

What is a worksheet?

Most house cleaners do not use worksheets so if you use one, you will immediately set yourself apart from all of the other house cleaners out there. It is a marketing tool, a progress report, your business card, your invoice and receipt.

Below you will see two pages of a three page worksheet. I've been using this exact same 3 page worksheet for 24 years and I still use it to this day because it works.

1. It works because it has your contact information at the top. (Look in the top header, there's your name, your slogan, your logo, your phone number and your email address) If your clients ever need to get in touch with you, all your information is right there on the page.

2. It works because you will show your clients on your initial walk through how you normally operate your business. You show them your work sheet and explain you will be filling one out each time you come to clean. Then have them walk you through their house and make notes on your worksheet about areas in their home that need special attention. Because you are making notes and filling in the blanks, you will know when you come back, which room was Megan's room,

or which room was Alex's room. You've made notes that the cat is named Whisper and the dog is named Melancholy. This information you will transfer to your client contact info in your cell phone once you are done with today's cleaning.

3. The check boxes allow you to inspect your own work, so there is never any guesswork what you have done while you are cleaning a home. You know what you have done, and so do they. As you do your final inspection, if you've forgotten anything, your check list will remind you.

4. Bottom of page 1, there is a place to write your return time, so you can book the next visit at your client's house before you ever leave. This is also where you determine if you are hired on an ongoing basis. If they set a return time for you that means they liked you and your work, and you're hired.

5. There are not "EXACT" titles for the rooms, say the house doesn't have an office but it does have a music room. Just cross out the office and write in "music room" so you both know what room you're talking about.

Page 2 has more rooms and is very similar to page 1, and all of the same rules apply to pages 2 that apply to page 1.

Click the link below for a free copy of the 3 page worksheet that you can edit and use immediately. Again, don't reinvent the wheel or spend all day doing graphic design. This is a proven and tested worksheet and works for everyone in our network. Work smart not hard --and get your business off the ground ASAP.

Yes. Send me free "Worksheets" that I can edit and use immediately. http://savvycleaner.com/worksheets

6. The Notes section on page 3 allows room for you to make a note. Use the Notes section to keep your clients in the loop of your plans or things you've noticed.

7. The supplies section is for special needs (supplies you normally don't carry).

8. It works because as you explain your worksheet – it walks you right through the rules and regulations and it answers most of the questions they might be asking. It makes the sales process easy. It makes you look professional.

House Cleaning from Life Long ...*So you can enjoy the most important things in life.*
Angela Brown / 555-555-5555 / Angela@AngelaBrown.com

NOTES about this weeks (or next week's) cleaning:

Your garden looks awesome!

6

7

SUPPLIES (Things we need for next time):

We need Draino for Megan's bathroom.

8

SPECIAL OR MISCELLANEOUS PROJECTS:
I work by the hour, so miscellaneous projects are welcome. Simply email or text me with your special requests so we can budget them in to our regular work routine. If we have to trade off – skip a room of your house in order to accommodate the special project, let me know which room(s) you are trading for.

WORK HOURS:
My normal workdays are Monday through Friday 8:00 a.m. to 6:00 p.m. I do work from a schedule and recommend the same time and weekday for your cleaning to create consistency and convenience for us both.

ALARM SYSTEMS & KEYS:
It is not necessary to be at home while I'm there cleaning. If you have an alarm, make sure I have the key code so I can disarm the alarm when I arrive, and set it again when I leave. I'll need to know where you keep your house key.

RESCHEDULING:
Stuff is going to happen. At one point or another -- for whatever reason, one of us, you or me is going to need to reschedule our cleaning. Communication is key. Call, text or email as soon as you know there is a conflict and we'll do our best to reschedule your cleaning at the next earliest convenience. I will do the same.

SICK POLICY:
If you or your children get sick with a contagious illness (i.e. the flu, a cold, pneumonia, chicken pox etc.) please call and reschedule your cleaning. Even though I disinfect your house, it is possible that I might transport germs to the next house or become sick myself. And to be fair to all of my customers I prefer to wait until you are well again. On my end, I may call in sick as well to protect you and your family.

SATISFACTION:
We aim to please. If for any reason, at any time you are not 100% completely satisfied, please call us immediately at 980-254-0900 and we will do everything in our power to resolve your concerns or your money back.

9

PAYMENT: Paying with a credit/debit card, or electronic check through PayPal is secure (and preferred) and leaves an electronic accounting trail for your records. Simply log on to paypal at: www.PayPal.com and click **Send Money,** then send to: **Angela@AngelaBrown.com,** the amount of today's services $ _100_ , **Goods and Services** and click send. Cash and Checks are also fine and can be left on the kitchen counter – or you can mail them to me at: Angela Brown, PO Box 49266, Charlotte NC 28277

Paid Cash. Thanks!

THANK YOU FOR YOUR BUSINESS!

9. The PAYMENT section bottom of page 3 walks you seamlessly through how you expect to be paid. And how they can send money via Pay-Pal if they forget to pay you. There is also a place there where you can write in the amount they've paid, and below it write the check number or make a note if they have paid you with cash and a handwritten note that simply says: "Paid. Thanks!" This PAYMENT section becomes their invoice or their receipt.

10. Your worksheet is an amazing referral tool. It has everything on it that somebody needs to know about your business. When your client is asked who cleans their house, they will get this worksheet and pass it along to their friends. (Remember your contact information is at the top — and all the stuff you do is listed, and all your rules are right here — and remember most house cleaning companies don't use worksheets — so Bam! You just made it really super easy for somebody to refer you, and easy for somebody to hire you.

What Should You Charge?

This is not a trick question. You have to determine as a business owner what you will charge each of your clients to go clean their houses – and you have to make enough money to stay in business.

All of your research on the internet will encourage you to charge by the job not by the hour. The theory for this is that you are going to buy into a franchise for $25,000 to $80,000 dollars, and pay 10% of your monthly gross in residuals to the franchisor, and then hire lots of people to work under you.

If you charge by the hour, your workers will work slow and stretch out the job to take longer -- so they will get paid more for less work. Because you have franchise fees and co-op advertising to pay for, you need to earn more money because you have rented warehouse space for all of your cleaning supplies, the expense of the cleaning supplies for all of your employees, vacuums and vacuum repair, vehicles and vehicle maintenance costs, gasoline, insurance premiums on the bonding and insurance of your employees, workman's comp, employee withholding tax, vehicle leases, payroll and so on.

The day will come when you will decide if you want to purchase a franchise and hire lots of people, but that is not today.

Today you are a one man or one woman show. You do not have a bunch of overhead expenses. You do not have employees and middle men.

You are on a program laid out to earn you $500 per week working part time or $1,000 a week full time. If you want to earn more, you can. You can work as many hours as you like.

The possibilities are endless and up to you and your work ethic.

This program was designed to be followed exactly, starting your business this week and by next week you'll have money coming in.

How much can I charge?
$25 per hour.

The range across the United States for independent house cleaners is $25-$45 per hour depending on the area you work in. Some of the more affluent areas charge on the higher side of that scale. You can charge more money if you have years of experience and you are incredible at cleaning houses.

DO NOT CHARGE MORE MONEY THAN $25 PER HOUR STARTING OUT.

If you don't have a proven track record, and you don't have references, and you don't have referrals -- and you come in charging more than $25 per hour – you better have some amazing cleaning skills to back it up, because the next house cleaner that comes by and undercuts your price will get you fired.

Having said that, if you run flyers that say you charge $25 per hour and you are bonded and insured and you offer a 100% satisfaction money back guarantee – that is enough for people to switch from their current house cleaner and give you a try. The secret is in your credentials, and the price you offer. Offering these WILL GET YOU THE JOB.

After that, it will be the quality of your work that will keep you employed.

If your prices keep changing, and you charge different amounts for similar houses, nobody can figure out what you charge, it makes recommending you more difficult, because you may be affordable to one client, and not affordable to another. Remember you don't want to pay for advertising, so keeping your pricing consistent let's your clients do the bidding for you. And you can work from referrals only.

There are so many reasons to charge by the hour. Here they are:

1. The math is super easy. Easy for you, easy for your clients, and easy for the clients to repeat and refer customers to you.

2. Charging by the hour allows you to block out your schedule by the hours you have available, rather than by the hours needed to complete the job.

3. Charging $25 is easy to budget. If you agree on a 3 hour time slot, each time you come to clean, you will work for 3 hours and you will be paid $75 regardless of how messy the house is. I promise there will be times when the house is twice as messy as other times, (after vacations, birthday parties, holidays, reunions, dinner parties etc.) and if you're working by the job, it will take you twice as long to clean. Don't fall into this trap.

4. Charging by the hour makes the client prioritize their cleaning needs, eliminating junk projects or daily chores they wouldn't pay for by the hour, but would leave to you, if you were simply cleaning the whole house. You will find that when you charge by the hour, your clients will clean up before you arrive, doing dishes, laundry, emptying trash and things that they can do, and just leave you to the deeper cleaning. This will streamline your actual cleaning and make your job easier. It will also save your clients money in the long run.

5. $25 bucks an hour makes it easy to figure out how many clients you need in order to pay your bills. How much money do you spend each month?

6. How many hours do you need to work? How many time slots can you create?

7. $25 bucks an hour will get you in any door, in any market. If you offer excellent cleaning at this price, I promise you, you will never lack for work.

At this rate, you can work five days per week x four hours a day and bring home $500 a week before taxes. That is $100 a day for part time work.

What jobs start you out from day one earning $25 bucks an hour? This is not money to be scoffed at – this is a really good wage for a few hours of work. Especially as a beginner.

Imagine a stay-at-home Dad who can't work a full time job, because his kids are in school six hours a day. Suppose he house cleans 4 hours a day in his neighborhood, and still has two hours per day to clean his own house, mow the yard, run errands and still pick up the kids from school on time, while pocketing an extra $500 a week. That is a cool $2,000 grand a month extra income.

Or how about a college student who doesn't go to school until 1:00pm each day? They could budget their time, going to bed earlier, and get up in time for an 8:00am to 12:00pm house cleaning and presto – suddenly they are paying off their student loans as they go. Can you imagine graduating college with no debt? *(And some business experience under your belt.)*

Suppose you decide to house clean as a full time job. You are starting from scratch today building your business and you decide to work two x 4 hour houses in a day. (5 days per week) That is $200 per day bring home pay before taxes, or $1,000 per week. The simple math is $4,000 per month (this does not consider cleaning supplies and gas for your car or travel time spent, so it is super important to work smart in order to keep the money you've earned.)

The key is creating a schedule, respecting your time and sticking to the schedule.

How to Bid a Job

Do I bid the job or does someone else?

Typically in a franchise the owner will go out and meet the prospective client face to face. They assess the home and the needs of the home (i.e. Does the family have pets, children, live in elderly parents, the general cleanliness of the home, the size of the home and the expectations presented.) They decide how much money it will cost to clean the entire home. They give a price based on the house, they do not charge by the hour.

Then they send somebody else out to clean it.

This is so wrong for so many reasons. Here's why:

The bidding process is the time where you bond with the prospective client. They determine if they like you, and you determine if you can work with them. When someone else does the bidding for you, they promise things they have no control over.

Then you, a different house cleaner than the one that did the bidding shows up, and the client has to start all over with building rapport. They don't trust this person, just because the house cleaner is new. The house cleaner is now trying to live up to expectations that don't come directly from the client – they heard it from their boss. Now the house cleaner has two bosses. The client – and the franchise owner. And the client feels tricked because there was a bait and switch. And this is typically how it works.

When *you* bid the job, you are promising the client directly what you can and can't do. You are setting the stage of realistic expectations. Take care not to over promise.

It's easy to over promise when you want the job, but you need to realize that you are human. You can only do so much. You may be the world's best house cleaner, but you don't ever want to be the one to say that. Don't set the bar so high you can't reach it. Or can't reach it consistently. The rule here is under promise and over deliver.

Be confident about your work, guarantee your work, offer a fair price, and be likeable. Be very clear about what you will and won't clean and clarify all the expectations up front.

Should I offer a free estimate?

You can, but if you're really good at selling you won't need to. When the prospective customer calls you on the phone, you can build rapport and establish their needs upfront without driving all the way over there.

The industry typically offers free estimates. So don't rule it out completely, because some people will insist – although I've bid one job in the last five years. I do it all over the phone in the initial consult which usually takes 3-5 min.

So what exactly is a free estimate?

It is where you get in your uniform, clean your car, print out a worksheet and drive to a prospective client's house...whom you've already established needs you to come clean. If you are going all the way over there in your uniform, why don't you assume you have the sale, and stay and clean while you are there?

- You have already determined that they need cleaning.
- We are going to assume that they don't know, like or trust you.
- You have to build trust and confidence and this usually takes a cleaning or two anyway. Why not get through that first hurdle today?

Charging $25 bucks an hour removes the need for "bidding jobs." You'll get a call and a prospective client will ask you to come bid a job. Here's the great part – you can simply say:

"I don't normally bid jobs. I'd be happy to come look at your house and I charge $25 per hour, regardless of the condition of your home, so it will just come down to your budget and your priorities.

Were you thinking of a one-time cleaning or do you need on-going cleaning?

(Chances are this person is calling you because they heard about you from a friend, or your flyer that has your price on it. The price is not a surprise to them. If they don't know about the $25 per hour, this is at the bottom of the normal rate going scale – so there will be no sticker shock. This is a really fair price to charge.)

I have one four hour slot open for $100 on Wednesday from 8:00-12:00 – I could swing by, meet you, and then stay and clean your house. Don't worry, I'm bonded and insured and I guarantee all of my work with a 100% satisfaction guarantee. So this gives you a chance to try me out with no risk. At the end of my cleaning if you don't like what I've done, there will be no charge.

If you do like me and my work, we'll pull out our schedules, and find a weekly, bi-weekly or monthly slot that works for both of us. Sound fair?

Do you want me to put you down for Wednesday (and include the date)?

Great, Wednesday (Date) at 8:00am sharp. I'll have you walk me through the house when I get there, show me your priorities and then once we're done with that, I'll start the clock for 4 hours. This first cleaning with the walkthrough will last till about 12:30pm and if you like my work will cost $100, if you don't like it, no charge.

I do bring all of my own supplies, but prefer to use your vacuum so I'm not transferring dust or germs from anyone else's house. Do you have a vacuum?

Awesome.

What is your address?

Great, thanks, and remind me of your last name...Thanks. *(Verify the spelling as you write it down.)*

And is this is the best number to text you?

Let me repeat that back: *(repeat it back)* *Thanks.*

Okay, great, I will text you on Tuesday to remind you I'm coming on Wednesday and I'll will see you Wednesday (date) at 8:00am sharp.

Really quickly you've bought back an hour of your time, that you would have spent on doing a free estimate. (Getting dressed, commute time and bidding the job.) Nobody gets paid for free estimates – so don't do them if you can help it.

What Type of Car Do I Need?

Is one car better than another?

The good news is that just about any working car that is clean will do the trick. Over the years I've had Hondas and those have served me well for house cleaning. You need enough space in the trunk for your cleaning supplies and if you decide to tote around a vacuum, you will want to be able to fit one in your car. I drop the back seats and lay a vacuum across the dropped space. Works just fine.
Other than that – any car will do.

Your car is an extension of your company image – so you will want the nicest car you can afford that fits the house cleaning image. By that I mean, you don't want to arrive for house cleaning in a car that is more expensive and luxurious than the cars your clients drive – this sends a mixed message that you are charging "too much" for your services. And you don't want your clients to have to play "keeping up with the Joneses" with you. They won't hire you if they feel inferior to you.

House cleaning is a blue collar job – and like an actor, you want to show up in character, with the right clothes, the right tools and the right type of car. Think mid-range $15,000-$30,000 (when new) compact or sedan, 8 years old or newer. Clean.

Upgrade your car

If your current car doesn't fit that image – upgrade as soon as you can afford to do so. Your company vehicle will be a tax deduction – so keep track of all of your mileage, and if you are making a car payment, because you are using it for business.

If you are driving an old rattle trap of a car, consider trading it in for one that is not falling apart or is missing a fender. You don't want your clients wondering about your safety, or your ability to get your fender fixed etc. Your clients hire you because they want to feel like they are in good hands, and you are going to take care of them. They do not want to feel like they are placing their home (their most valuable asset) in the hands of a dangerous person (driver) who is careless (the accident you were obviously in, could have been your fault, and they may assume you don't give a flip about the consequences or getting it fixed.) How you take care of your own stuff sends a message of how you will take care of theirs.

If you are driving an old beat up car that is duct taped together and you can't afford to upgrade it now – address it on your initial walk through. When you meet the customer for the first time, address it briefly. (You know your customers will be wondering about the type of person they are hiring) *and you need to answer that question in simple terms.*

"I'm so thrilled to be cleaning your house, I'm working through some personal goals and one is to upgrade my car, so I'm so blessed you called me."

Do NOT go into any more details than this, do not explain why your car is a piece of crap -- and do not make your personal drama your client's drama. (They don't need to know your wife left you and all you got was this beat up car and hefty alimony payments.)

Unlimited car wash

In the section on "Image", we address the beauty of belonging to an unlimited car wash. I have my husband signed up at Auto bell and my cleaning car is signed up at SamsXpress. Both car wash services range from $25 - $29 per month and offer unlimited drive through car washes. The cost is equivalent to one hour of my house cleaning time, and saves me far more time than if I were to clean the cars myself with a garden hose and a bucket of soapy water. Fortunately for me, the car wash I use is in the same parking lot as Walmart where I buy my cleaning supplies so it's convenient. The car washes also have a way of processing and recycling the water used to wash my car – and I don't have that luxury when doing it with a garden hose.

However, when I arrive to clean a house – Any house, at any time, my car is sparkly -- and it is a reflection of the services I offer.

I was cleaning in a neighborhood the other day and there was an independent house cleaner (not a franchised company) with a mucked up car, filthy and had misspelled window stickers advertising house cleaning. My first thought was this: "You can't take care of your own stuff, how on earth are you going to take care of mine?" My first initial impression was judgmental – and inside could have been the most amazing house cleaner, but I was turned off by the first impression – and I'm rooting for house cleaners. I was on her/his side. Don't be that guy or girl.

Take pride in your company image and the image of your car. It's a cost of advertising that pays handsomely.

The Importance of Being on Time

I'm the boss, I set the hours right?

You are your own boss so theoretically you get to set your own hours. I'll make it really easy on you.

Set a schedule and stick to it and you will never lack for work.

This is such an easy thing to do and this is the Achilles heel where all independent house cleaners fall apart. They think that since they get to set the hours, they have all the flexibility in the world – you do. And you don't.

When a client is expecting you and you don't show, your client loses confidence in you. If you are supposed to show up at 8:00am and they are not comfortable giving you a house key, but they stay home from work to let you in – and you don't show up until 9:00 you've made them late for work and before you even start cleaning, they are ticked with you.

It helps if you are an amazing house cleaner, but if you just show up on time, every time – you will be so far ahead of all the other house cleaners out there. It's a no brainer. Set a time to show up -- and show up on that time.

Being punctual is part of your reputation and it is one of the things that will promote your business or kill it before you ever get started.

In twenty four years of cleaning houses, the biggest reason for people hiring me is this: "My last house cleaner was unreliable. I never knew when she was coming."

That's it? She/he was honest, hardworking, did a great job, reasonable pricing whatever, but didn't show up on time so they were replaced? Wow. That is a very easy fix.

Finding new customers costs a lot of time and energy. It is way easier to be reliable and keep the customers you have.

Your schedule should allow for a few minutes between houses, which gives you time to repack your cleaning caddy in your car, eat a quick bite of lunch or drink a smoothie to keep up your energy between houses, drive to your next house, and then sit in your car for five to six minutes, return calls, check email and review notes about the next client (pets names, kids names, client hot buttons, priorities, special requests etc.) and confirm tomorrow's house cleaning appointments via text.

Then three minutes before the scheduled time, you pull into the drive, unpack your car and be on their porch, ringing the doorbell exactly at the time they are expecting you.

EVERY SINGLE TIME.

You know what they tell their friends? "You can set your clock by her/his arrival time."

We all have 24 hours in a day. You and your clients. When you show up on time, you are saying: *"Hey I respect your time and I value my own."* If you value your own time, your clients will value it as well.

So if you are charging by the hour – you want your hour to begin and end on time. This is as important for you as it is for your client. If you are sloppy with your time, you will waste a lot of it, or give time away free, and time is money. So set a schedule, and stick to the schedule.

Everybody else operates on schedules, the airlines, your doctors, the schools, other jobs you may have – there is a time you are expected to show up, and this is the same.

You can even offer an on time guarantee. If you are late, your first hour is free. That will set a fire under you to always be on time.

So what happens if I'm late?

When you are late your client is unconsciously or consciously thinking: What happened to my house cleaner? They're late.

- Did they get in an accident?
- Did they forget about me?
- Are they still at someone else's house?
- Is that client more important than me?
- Don't they respect my time?

A series of questions goes through their heads that makes them question the decision they made to hire you.

If for some strange reason you are late, text your client. Let them know you're running 15 minutes late.

And make sure you text them before you are supposed to arrive. Don't text them after your expected arrival time. Keep them in the loop. Communicate with your clients and you will always have clients.

Texting your clients will remind them that you are in fact reliable – because you cared enough to text – and you are grown up enough to take responsibility for some rare, unforeseen situation that caused you to be late.

Confidence Builders

Confidence is crucial to your success as the owner of a house cleaning company.

When you talk to your clients, they expect you to be an expert. They are hiring you because you solve problems. Problems of organization, messy and cluttered houses. They expect you will clean their homes and make them sparkly and smell nice. They expect you to know how to clean, how to budget your time, and what chemicals to use on various surfaces.

How do I become an expert at cleaning houses?

- By cleaning houses.
- By learning everything there is to know about house cleaning.
- By adding certifications to your resume.
- By networking with colleagues and industry peers.
- By attending house cleaning webinars to learn tips and tricks to troubleshoot and grow your business.
- By correcting course when you screw up.

Things malfunction all the time on jobs, you will run out of supplies, you will lock yourself out of people's houses, you will irritate small animals, kids will get in your way, you will bump plants that will knock over and make a mess, and you will bang your head on weirdly placed objects on the walls.

As you learn to navigate these "normal" issues in house cleaning, the drama from them dwindles and it's not a big deal. Big whoop. You can handle anything...and that builds confidence.

Other confidence builders

If you are terribly shy and don't like talking to people, or feel uncomfortable about making eye contact and speaking up when talking to clients, or you are not sharp when thinking on your feet, consider joining Toastmasters International.

It is a public speaking group that costs about $30 to join for a six month membership and has weekly meetings. The meetings are filled with supportive people and a scheduled agenda that walks you through the basics of presenting yourself in public. Things you will learn and practice in Toastmasters are:

1. Eye Contact
2. Speaking in Sincerity
3. Using hand gestures
4. Mastering facial gestures
5. Body language
6. Vocal Variety
7. Thinking on your feet

And so much more. Toastmasters is a world-wide non-profit organization that has benefitted more CEO's, salespeople, managers, bosses, housecleaners, maids and janitors than any other single organization on the planet. Employees who join Toastmasters skyrocket to the top of their fields because of the confidence personally and professionally that it builds.

Check out a club near you and attend just one meeting. (You'll be hooked – it totally rocks.) www.Toastmasters.org

The secret is you may be insecure, and that is okay. But when you show up to meet a client, and to clean their home, you are an actor. You are the CEO of a boutique residential cleaning service and you need to wear that title with confidence and pride.

Confidence and pride are contagious. If you have it and you share it, your clients will catch it and pass it along through referrals of you.

How Do I Build Credentials?

I don't even have any references yet!

Excellent question. Your credentials are the reasons people will or won't hire you. If you are just starting out and you don't have any credentials you will need to answer some basic questions up front that will remove the fear of someone bringing you into their home.

Do you have references?

References are a good way to build credentials, but if somebody asks if you have them and you don't -- be honest. Say:

"I cannot provide any references at this time." (Pause for dramatic effect. This is so disarming, and honest that what you say next will cement your sale.) ***"But I'd love one from you. I do offer a 100% money-back, satisfaction guarantee and here's how it works: I come clean your home, and when I'm done I will have you inspect my work. If you do not like for any reason, the work I have done, you don't owe me a dime. If when I'm done, I pass your inspection, you pay me, we set a regular schedule for me to return, and you write me a reference I can share with your neighbors." Deal?"***

And you say this with a smile on your face and with utmost confidence. I've never run into a person with all of the people I've trained, who didn't land the deal.

Do you offer a satisfaction guarantee?

Yes. I recommend you do – it will help you lock in a client who may be afraid to take a risk on somebody they don't know.

Your satisfaction guarantee can be whatever you want it to be. I recommend an iron clad, 100% money back, satisfaction guarantee. If for whatever reason your client is not completely satisfied with the work you have done, you refund their money.

This does three things:

> 1. It forces you to do your best work, every time you go clean a house.

> 2. It shows the client you're not messing around, and you stand behind your work.

> 3. It will bring you more referrals when clients brag to their friends about how you operate.

In twenty four years of cleaning, I've had one client get their money back and it was because she didn't clear the new house cleaning expense first with her husband who managed the family finances. When he returned home he said they couldn't afford a house cleaner since they were in so much debt – and to keep peace in their family I insisted there was no charge. They fought over it because she wanted to pay me something and he wanted to pay off debts first. I left quickly as not to get involved in the family dynamics and she ended up sending me a bunch of referral business.

Are you bonded & insured?

You will be asked if you are bonded and insured. Choose to be both bonded and insured. It protects you and your client. It costs about $30 a month for both premiums and it lends instant credibility.

This is an activity you can do today. Call the insurance company and get signed up for bonding and insurance. They will ask you for your company name or if you are doing business as yourself. They will also ask you for the specifics of your job. NOTE: You are looking for housecleaning or janitorial coverage.

If you advertise that you are bonded and insured, it looks like you know what you are doing. If you are not familiar with bonding and insurance, check out the section in this book on "Bonding and Insurance".

Bonding and insurance is a deal breaker for most people. House cleaning is a really competitive business and there are a hundred people who are bonded and insured waiting in line for your clients. Don't lose business because you don't understand the importance of it, or are too cheap to buy it.

What are your training credentials?

This is where you list which college you graduated from to get into house cleaning.

Just Kidding.

It is where you list how you have been trained to clean houses. When you pay $25,000 - $80,000 to buy into a house cleaning franchise, you are attaching your name to existing credentials and you learn their marketing and "How to Clean" systems.

As the owner of an independent house cleaning company you will be creating your own credentials and you can do this by scouring the internet and learning everything you can about house cleaning, reading Pinterest pages or blogs and hoping it all works. That's what I did when I got started and it took me 8 years of trial and error to figure it all out. LOL *(Don't be me.)*

Or you can join a world-wide recognized training program like the one offered at http://www.savvycleaner.com/ and find all the training you need in one place. It is super affordable compared to a franchise and carries as much weight.

Do you have any certifications?

By going through the online Savvy Cleaner® program, you will become trained and Savvy Cleaner Certified® and you can proudly say you are. You can explain to your clients that you have been trained by the world's largest and most comprehensive on-line training program for independent house cleaners and that you understand and meet all of the OSHA standards for house cleaners.

Do you belong to any networks or organizations?

You can join your local chamber of commerce, https://www.uschamber.com Better Business Bureau https://www.bbb.org/ and Angie's List www.angieslist.com (those three are not necessarily going to help you – but will give you instant credibility.)

Once Savvy Cleaner Certified®, you can join the Savvy Cleaner Network® which is a private, community of other house cleaners who troubleshoot industry issues, and support each other, and attend live/ongoing trainings.

Your continual training and support is paramount to many home owners. Your clients want to know that people who are coming in their home to maintain their most valuable asset, (their home) are on the cutting edge of information.

On your flyer, you will want to list your "hiring" credentials. These are the reasons someone should hire you.

- You offer an excellent service that everybody needs
- At an affordable price
- With the assurance of proper training
- Ongoing training and support

- Satisfaction guarantee
- Backed by bonding and insurance
- And...you accept credit cards.

This answers enough of the questions that you will book 99% of the jobs you are called for. Congratulations! Now you have the credentials you need for your new house cleaning business.

Bonding and Insurance

Are you bonded?

Translation: *If you commit fraud, or steal from me will I be reimbursed?*

Do you need a bond? If you are honest, no. But your new clients don't know this and they don't know you. And when they hire you, they are inviting a perfect stranger into their home. They have valuables, they have children and they have pets. They have expensive cars and expensive stuff.

A bond protects your customers in case of theft. Here's how it works. Let's say you cleaned a house and the customer later finds his Rolex watch is missing from the bathroom sink and they think you took it. So they file a police report. The police come to your house and investigate, and if they find proof you took it, you are going to have return it, or replace the watch if you've pawned or fenced it. If you have to replace the watch and don't have the money, the bond would pay the client to replace the Rolex watch. Once the bond is paid out, you then repay the bond in installments. Either way – if you steal it, or an employee of yours steals it – you have to pay to reimburse the client. So hope you never have to use it, but it brings great peace of mind to use this in your advertising.

Lots of people will ask you if you are bonded and insured. Lots of house cleaners lie. Don't do it. If you say "yes, you have bonding and insurance," be prepared to tell them which company you are bonded through.

Because the next question that follows is "With which company?" You are paying $30 per month to an insurance company for bonding and insurance, you should have an answer that flows really quickly off the end of your tongue.

Answer: **Nationwide, would you like the number of my policy for verification?**

If you can't provide the answers to these questions, you shouldn't be in someone else's home.

NOTE:

Don't bring anyone with you into the house that is not bonded and insured. Let's say your sister comes to visit and she does not own a house cleaning company and is not bonded and insured, can she help you clean for the day? The answer is no.

She may be the best house cleaner in the world, but without the bonding and insurance, you are not protected and neither is the house owner.

Can your teenage daughter come help you clean or your husband? Not unless they are bonded and insured.

My mom came to visit for a couple of weeks and didn't want to stay home while I was house cleaning during the day. She offered to come help me.

AWESOME – I could really have used her help. But wait! She wasn't bonded or insured so I had to leave her home.

Guess what? My mom is the most trustworthy person on the planet. I know that. My clients however, do not. They don't know my mom. I couldn't bring her along.

Are you insured?

Translation: *If you don't know what you're doing and you ruin the finish on my hardwood floors and I have to have them refinished or replaced can you pay for it?*

Insurance is vital. You want to use the fact that you are insured in your advertising. Insurance for your client's property is a good business move, as it protects you from crazy clients who may try to sue you for ruining a finish on stainless steel appliances or breaking a valuable heirloom.

If anything should happen to your clients property – your fault or not, if they blame you, you are responsible. So yes, get insurance.

Note: One reason we choose houses in the 0-15 year range is the hardwood floors are coated in a different resin than they were say twenty or thirty years ago. Cleaning them is easier and doesn't require waxes and shines that older floors do. If you use a wax on a newer floor, you can ruin the hardwood beyond repair and some of these 3,000-5,000 square foot homes have enormous amounts of hardwood. Replacing them could be $27,000-$63,000. You don't want that kind of out of pocket expense.

If you decide to join us at Savvy Cleaner http://savvycleaner.com we'll teach you everything you need to know about every type of surface and what chemicals you can and CANNOT use.

If you decide to go the free route and figure it out yourself, really spend some time and do your homework learning this stuff before you start cleaning.

I would hate it for you if you ruined somebody's granite counter top, or leather furniture because you just didn't know any better.

Trust me, I've heard all of the stories and they are NOT pretty. VERY expensive to replace and repair and it's happened to some of the nicest people I know.

What the heck is a Mulligan?

What is a Mulligan?

(Description from Wikipedia)

A mulligan is a second chance to perform an action, usually after the first chance went wrong through bad luck or a blunder. Its best-known meaning is in golf whereby a player is informally allowed to replay a stroke (though this is against the formal rules of golf). The term has also been applied to other sports and games, and to other fields generally. The origin of the term is unclear.

How do you play the Mulligan game?

As a long term house cleaner, I've been part of a network of other house cleaners that compare notes, offer suggestions and peer support. For years we've been playing the Mulligan game – and you can too. We are using the term Mulligan as a "doing something extra that needs to be done, (being given a second chance) that is not part of what you are being paid to do, or going the second mile." And you can never mention it to your client, or other clients for whom you clean.

Here are the rules: After all of your work is done and you are ready to leave the client's house, if you have a moment to spare, what one additional thing can you do on your way out the door, that will be noticed immediately and will make the client smile when they notice? (The Mulligans get talked about at parties, bus stops and amongst neighbors while they are gossiping or bragging about their house cleaners. The Mulligan will bring you lots of referral business.) Work them into your schedule if you can. Think of it as doing a kind deed on your way home.

Your Mulligan should take no longer than 10 minutes at most and is a gift. You do NOT charge for this bonus.

Example Mulligans:

- Bringing in the trash can on garbage day that is out on the curb.
- Watering droopy house plants that have been neglected.
- Cleaning the inside glass of a china hutch (that you normally don't clean)
- Organizing a toy box or game shelf
- Scrubbing an electric toothbrush that has muck on the charging station.
- Cleaning front door porch lights.
- Scrubbing out the animal food and water dishes.
- Refilling the Q-tips jar or the toilet paper holders.

The list has endless possibilities and you will usually be cleaning and see "something else" that needs to be clean (often falls in the category of deep cleaning) and you have to move on in order to be done in time. So you come back to this as your last stop if you can possibly arrange it. Mulligan accomplished!

How to Get Referrals

Should you ask for referrals?

This one is up to you. Some of the independent house cleaners in thy Savvy Cleaner Network® do ask for referrals, and some advertise they offer referral fees. It depends entirely on how you feel about the referral process.

Personally, I prefer not to ask for referrals, and I don't advertise I will pay a referral fee to someone who gives me one. (I do pay a referral fee, but I don't advertise it.)

To me it seems somehow manipulative to ask for referrals, and I don't want my clients sticking their neck out for me, unless it is genuine and a referral is how they really feel about me.

Your client will feel very differently, and show a greater enthusiasm about you and the cleaning service you provide, if they decide to recommend you all on their own, than they will if you ask or bribe them.

How to get referrals

1. If you are good at what you do – you will get referrals.
2. If the client feels you offer a good product at a fair price – you will get referrals.
3. If you show up on time, on the day you have scheduled – you will get referrals.

4. If you are efficient cleaning house – you will get referrals.
5. If you treat the client's property and animals with respect – you will get referrals.
6. If something goes awry and you handle it professionally – you will get referrals.
7. If you are confidential and don't blab to the neighbors about your clients – you will get referrals.

We live in an era where everyone is seems has home security cameras. How you clean, how you treat their stuff, how you treat their animals is all caught on camera, and your client could be watching you remotely from their smart phone or tablet.

ASSUME you are always being watched when you clean.

So are you asking for referrals? No. You are earning them. Earning a referral is far more powerful than asking will ever be.

If you get a referral should you pay a referral fee?

Yes. See the next section on "Referral Fees" to determine appropriate money and gifts. I don't want to go off on a tangent to talk about that here – I really want to talk about how you *get* referrals.

So you are just starting out your business and you will be running flyers until you get your business off the ground. From day one until your last day in business - work this phrase into your conversation:

"I work by referral only." If you are just starting out and you don't have any clients, you are expanding in the area so you are doing a one time, initial introduction to your company, but you work by referral only.

For the dozens of times I've relocated and started a house cleaning company in a new area and I've done the initial flyer run I've included this phrase on my flyers in small print at the bottom.

Hi I'm Angela Brown and I'm your new neighbor. Learn more about me and my services at: www.AngelaBrown.com **I've owned a professional house cleaning company for several years and I'm *really good* at what I do.**

I'm consistent, I'm reliable, and I'm flexible and efficient.

- **If you don't need my service today, save this until you do. This is a one-time only introduction as I relocate. *I work by referral only.***

Now you have just created a sense of scarcity – this is a one-time only introduction, so people WILL save your flyer...and call you now, or later. You just said you won't be running anymore flyers. This also suggests you expect to be super busy with your new referrals, and somehow confident enough not to have to run flyers a second time. Bravo! You've just painted a picture of elitism.

You also mentioned that you work by referral only - which suggests you offer a premium service worthy of a referral.

In the world of house cleaners – there are not many who *can or will* say they work by referral only. Your saying so set's you apart from all the others, including franchises that spend thousands each year on advertising.

You are a small business – a one man or woman show at this point, and you have complete control over the work you do.

Work so people can't help but referring you. It will save you thousands in advertising.

And here's the truth, if your schedule is filled to the maximum (20-30 houses) you don't need to spend thousands of dollars on advertising. It's not cost effective in any way to pay to advertise, as a one man/woman house cleaner.

If you are sloppy, lazy or unreliable, you will HAVE to pay for advertising to keep new business coming in. The referral system is WAY CHEAPER and far more effective than any advertising you will ever pay for. Remember that.

If people know you work by referral only...when they talk about you -- They say what they know, which is: you work by referral only. It's powerful stuff – like it or not, you teach your clients up front how to promote you by the image you project, and by the subtle things you say.

Should You Pay a Referral Fee?

Yes. You should reward the clients who believe in you enough to send more business your way. Think of it as a marketing cost. *We are not talking about paying money for leads on HomeAdvisor.com or Angie's list listings, or Yellow Page ads, Yelp or Yext listings. And we're not talking about you advertising in neighborhood penny savers, bargain hunter newspapers or mailing services like ValPak.* Save your money and use it to reward people who already like you and have referred business to you.

Psychology 101 tells us that the behavior we reward (or pay attention to) is repeated. So yes, you want to make sending referrals your way a positive experience that your client will want to repeat.

Your clients like to be rewarded, acknowledged and appreciated. Clients like to feel like they are getting a good deal. Clients like to recommend services that make them feel like they made a good choice. The good news is, when you positively reinforce the behavior of sending you referrals...they will send you more referrals. Soon your schedule will be so full you will never look back.

You can do one of three things, you can pay cash. You can give extra house cleaning time, or you can give a gift.

How much should you pay for a referral?

This depends entirely on how big the referral was. Were you given a single house cleaning opportunity such as a "move out" referral? If so, you want to give something that says "Thank you, I appreciate what you have done for me." This may be the equivalent to an hour of your cleaning time, or a small plant or perhaps a showerhead on a hose that will make your future house cleaning easier. ($25-$35 value).

If you were referred continual business say a bi-weekly client who now uses your services twice a month, a bigger gift of two or three house cleaning hours would be appropriate. ($50-$75 value).

If a client advertises for you – at their expense (either with paid advertising, or their reputation, say posting and recommending you and your services, you're your phone number and email, on a neighborhood site like "NextDoor" http://www.nextdoor.com or a neighborhood Facebook group page, you will pick up five or ten new clients – then an even bigger gift the equivalent of one or two entire cleanings would be appropriate. ($75-$200 Value).

I cap my waiting list at 30 people. Why? Because my clients never go away. They move and they lose their jobs, but they don't randomly fire me or quit. So there is very little attrition or turn over in my business. I will never get to clean for the 30 people on my waiting list.

So what happens to other people who call? In 2015 while cleaning houses, I had a client post a lovely recommendation on **NextDoor** http://www.nextdoor.com which is a neighborhood app that is like **MyNeighborhood** http://www.myneighborhood.com where neighbors can recommend house cleaners, handy men, landscapers, plumbers, or private contractors that you have had a positive experience with.

Oddly enough, because misery loves company, and so do glowing recommendations from delighted clients – my clients in two neighborhoods gave dueling recommendations of me, trying to out-do, or one-up each other with their praises for me in a public forum where lots of my other clients are members. I was the talk of the neighborhood for a minute, and my phone went ballistic.

Unfortunately for me, I was already running a cleaning schedule at full capacity.

I gave away 40 to 50 new prospective clients a month for four or five months.

I personally interviewed other house cleaners in the area, I wanted to know how much they charged. How they worked, how they knew what chemicals to use on various surfaces. Where they bonded and insured? Were they honest? Were they reliable? What training did they have in house cleaning? How long had they been in business? What were their credentials?

The ones that really inspired me – I sent all of the new business their way. It cost me nothing, except a few minutes of my time, and it provided excellent customer service to people I most likely would never get to work with. Those people however, would still communicate with the existing clients I have, who recommended me on the community page in the first place.

Here's what I did:

(I returned the phone calls and texts from prospective clients with a note that said: *"Hey John, I work by referral only, so I'm thrilled and blessed that you called. However my schedule is booked to capacity, and in order to serve my existing clients, I am unable to accept any new business at this time.*

However, Irene is another independent house cleaner in the area that I've recently interviewed and I'd love to pass along her contact information. She's really great at house cleaning, she's organized, she's bonded and insured, and she'll really do a great job for you. Her number is: 000-000-0000. Tell her Angela Brown sent you."

So I didn't ever get to work with the incoming clients, but the short interaction with them was a vetted recommendation for another house cleaner. All of the new prospective clients were receptive to the new recommendations I passed along.

And existing clients I had, commented later while I was cleaning their houses that they heard from neighbors that my schedule was booked, yet they were impressed I took the time to find their friends and neighbors a house cleaner.

So in a sense, it was another way of not making my existing customer (who had sent me the referral) look bad in front of their friends.

When you honor the referral system, it honors you back.

Billing & Collections

How do I get paid?

You get paid when you clean a house. The client will usually leave a check or cash on the kitchen counter for you with your name on it.

This is one of the biggest perks of starting your own house cleaning company. You don't have to wait for payroll to send you a check, or the two weeks lots of people have to wait until pay day.

You just have to train your clients to pay you each time you come.

When you are doing your initial walk through with the client, and you have your clip board and worksheets in hand, there is a moment when you cover payments.

You'll want to say these exact words – simply because they work: (Please memorize them and practice them until they seamlessly roll off your tongue with finesse.)

"I accept checks, cash and all major credit cards as well as PayPal – whichever is easier for you. Usually people leave a check on the kitchen counter and I pick it up after I've cleaned.

I'm not a collection agency, and I'm not set up to go chasing after money I've earned. I don't send invoices or receipts – but I do leave this worksheet with you each time I come. If you leave me a check, I will mark that I've received it right here (Show them the section that talks about payment), and if you forget, I'll just make a note of it here (same spot) and you can send the money via PayPal when you get home from work."

That will do the trick.

Should I leave and not clean a house if somebody forgets to pay?

Nope. You've confirmed with your client via text message, 24 hours in advance of your cleaning, so they know you are coming and they know they need to pay you for your service. You have booked that time for them – and if they haven't cancelled on you, they need to pay you.

If you arrive and there is no check, don't worry, they may return home before you are done cleaning and pay you cash or pay with a credit card.

You can't sell the time to someone else because you are already there. (This is the reason for confirming 24 hours in advance.)

Clean the house as you normally would and assume the money will arrive before you leave. Don't get weirded out and feel like you are doing a "free cleaning" or get all worked up in your head that they you're fired and they chose not to pay you.

All of your clients have complicated lives – that is why they hired you in the first place. They will pay you.

Should I hire a collection agency if somebody does not pay?

No. You are not a collection agency and you are not set up to go chasing after money you've earned. Plain and simple.

Because you will confirm each appointment before you arrive via text or email – this is a good time to remind them if they haven't paid you from last cleaning.

In twenty four years of cleaning, I have had a couple of clients forget to pay me and they paid me immediately upon remembering they forgot to pay. Either by PayPal, mailing a check, or running a check over and leaving it in my mailbox. People you have helped, who like you, who appreciate your service, don't try to cheat you out of your money.

- One of my clients only pays bills once every two weeks on payday. He asked in advance if he could pay on payday regardless of when I clean. He was a bi-weekly client so it turns out I clean his house twice a month on a schedule and he pays me twice a month on a different schedule, but we agreed to it in advance and he always pays.

The goal here is to always get paid for the work you do.

TANGENT RANT:

There is a really great girl in our network who for some reason refuses to use worksheets. She has no way of verifying the work she's done with the client and in turn the client's frequently "forgets" to pay her. When you use the worksheet, you're checking off the tasks you've completed so the client knows what you have done that day during your cleaning session. What you have checked off is what you are guaranteeing in your satisfaction guarantee for that day. It is also your invoice, a list of your rules and regulations (which clearly state that you need to be paid each visit, or paid that evening via PayPal – and the email address at which they can send you money.) Your worksheet is also your receipt where you make a note that you got paid, or you didn't.

I rant for this reason: She's an awesome house cleaner with a stupid hang-up. She won't use worksheets which could solve all of these problems. Here's what she does instead: (I provide private troubleshooting and consulting to housecleaners for a reasonable fee.) So she hires me again, and again calling me up crying because she didn't get paid. (This happens at least twice month.)

She doesn't like confrontation, so she doesn't want to ask the client for money, which eventually she has to. The client plays dumb and says *"come over to my office and pick up a check right now."* So she drives all the way across town (wasting her own time and gas money) and when she gets to the office, the client has just stepped out, leaving no check with the secretary.

Sadly, she is training her clients that she can be bullied. No offense to her personally, we all operate our own independent businesses differently, and as the boss you are free to operate yours any way you like. However, we have specific processes we've created over time that work. ALL of the other house cleaners in our network who use worksheets, never have this problem.

So how do you know when to "quit" a client for non-pay?

Follow these steps exactly:

1. You confirm your scheduled cleaning via text or email to the client 24 hours prior.

2. You show up for your cleaning and there is no money. You stay and clean.

3. On your worksheet, circle your email address and the PayPal section and the amount owed you for today's cleaning. (Let's suppose the client still doesn't pay.)

4. Next scheduled apt. confirm your scheduled cleaning via text or email to the client 24 hours prior, this time with a note saying you need to be

paid for last time and this time with a check for
_____ amount of dollars left on the counter
to ensure continued service.

5. You show up for your scheduled cleaning and there is still no money. (This is the second cleaning where you have confirmed, then showed up for your scheduled cleaning and there is no money.)

   - From the client's house, before you clean, call the client and have a conversation. Find out what is going on, has there been a family emergency? A loss of job, dissatisfaction of service? If it is possible, get a credit card number from the client and process it right then, via your Square account. https://squareup.com/

6. If you can't get the client on the phone, or if they refuse to give you their credit card, turn your worksheet over and write them a personal note on the blank page. Your personal note should be something like this:

Hey (Name),

I showed up to clean today, per our confirmed cleaning appointment, and noticed for a second time there was no money left for my service. I tried calling

you and couldn't get though, and am worried that something terrible has happened.

I hope you are okay. Please let me know that you are.

If the something terrible was my service, please let me know that as well, and I will do everything in my power to correct it.

I don't want to keep running up a tab on your account, so I didn't clean today. So no charge for today, just the ($100 or whatever the amount was) for last week's service is all that is owed, and you can send it to me via PayPal at (Your@emailaddress.com), I've also suspended your cleaning service until payment is received.

I do have a waiting list of clients who want your spot. So if you still want to keep your scheduled cleaning, please let me know a.s.a.p.

Thanks again for your business,

(Your Name)
(Your phone)
(Your email/PayPal Address)

7. And then leave. Don't call the client, don't harass them, let them make the next move. (They most likely will try to clear up what is going on.)

8. If you don't hear from them for a week, give their scheduled cleaning slot to another customer and don't look back. Consider the loss of money someone cashing in their money back guarantee and write it off as a business loss.

Payments

Your choice, but it is recommended that you accept cash, personal or business checks, PayPal and all major credit cards. Why?

Cash

Because there are people who only deal in cash. Lots of people who hire you will give you cash as payment. It is my least favorite of the payment forms because it is harder to keep track of and it leaves no paper trail.

When paid with cash, keep it in a secure place, until you pass by your bank and then make a lump deposit and mark the receipt as house cleaning money.

The old way of doing business was "getting paid under the table" meaning you did not report your earnings on your taxes. I do not recommend this method simply because you are setting yourself up to be audited at some point.

As a company owner, you want to set your business up correctly from the start. Report all of your earnings. Pay your taxes. Deduct your expenses.

It's super simple and will keep you in check with the law.

We live in a free country that allows us to be our own boss. We get to use public roads. We send our children to public schools. We have access to the US Postal system, public parks and libraries. We have public officials, police officers, fire departments and servicemen who fight for our freedoms and personal safety on a daily basis. These services are paid for with our tax dollars.

Please don't feel that you are above the law – you're not.

Every year there are famous and not-so-famous people that go to jail for tax fraud. Don't be a moron and go to jail because you are trying to save a few hundred or a few thousand bucks. It's just not worth it.

Checks

Checks are the preferred method for most house cleaners. Checks are simple, you have a record, the bank has a record, and your client has a record.

Bam! You're done. Well not quite.

You still have to deposit the check. Your bank may offer mobile banking and if they do, I highly recommend setting up your account so you can deposit your checks right from your smart phone. Even if you drive by several branches of your local bank each day, the time you will save pulling in to the bank, waiting in line behind another car and then the three to five minutes you will spend making sure the deposit went through really adds up day after day.

Train yourself when you unpack and repack your cleaning caddy to "close out" all of your accounts for the day. Make notes to yourself about special projects, client requests, mobile deposit their check on your smart phone, and make sure you've set a rescheduling time to return with the client. Bam! Now you're done.

PayPal

PayPal is linked to an email address and your bank account -- and is a convenient way for people to pay for your services. This is a fall back method for people who "forgot" to leave a check for your house cleaning.

With PayPal they can pay you with a credit card, or a check and the money goes into a storage account. You can manually log into PayPal and transfer the money into your bank account, or you can leave it in your PayPal account as a savings account for use at a later date.

NOTE: If a client wants to, they can set up recurring payments directly from PayPal so that they don't have to worry about writing you a check each time. Once you've agreed on a fixed price (say 4 hours x $100) the $100 auto deducts from their account and pays you on the schedule you've agreed on (weekly, bi-weekly, monthly etc.) They will get a receipt from PayPal each deduction, and you will get an email confirmation that you've been paid. It's super simple.

Accepting credit cards is a privilege once reserved for "merchants" only. As a merchant, you had a hefty monthly fee for the privilege of accepting credit cards along with a transaction fee which is usually 2.75% to 3.0% of the transaction. With PayPal, you pay the transaction fee, which is deducted automatically from the transaction, but hooray! There is no monthly merchant fee. The transaction fee is the cost of doing business. 97% of say $100 is better than no money at all. (And certainly cheaper than hiring a collection agency to send harassing letters or phone calls to your clients to collect money.)

Credit Cards

And just accepting credit cards as payment is also a brilliant idea since some of your clients don't have the money to pay you at all, and they are willing to finance your cleaning on a credit card, or they are collecting frequent flyer or other rewards points by purchasing everything, including house cleaning with a credit card.

Without a merchant account you can use a square reader that hooks right in to your cell phone and you can swipe a credit card with ease. https://squareup.com/ will show you how to get started.

Basically you create a square account and link your bank account. When money is deposited it goes directly into your account, minus the merchant fee or processing fee.

You can leave notes such as: "House Cleaning by Angela Brown" which is what will show on your client's credit card statement.

You can get the reader for $10 bucks, and often under various promotions the Square reader is free of charge. Check to see if they are running a current promotion.

If you do not have a reader, (I had one, but it accidentally went through the washing machine in my pants pocket and ruined it) you can manually enter the credit card information and then the client uses their finger to sign the purchase right there on the screen of your smart phone.

Accepting credit cards sometimes is the difference between landing a job or not. If you accept credit cards, and another competing house cleaner does not, you may be the one that gets the job. Hooray for you.

To Do This Week

You've arrived at the end of this book which means you are well on your way to starting your own house cleaning business. As a quick reminder here's what you need to do this week in order to have money coming in next week:

Day One:

1. Read this book from cover to cover.
2. Order uniforms (If you don't have money for 5-7 uniforms, at least get one and wash it each night.)
3. Download flyers, http://savvycleaner.com/flyers worksheets, http://savvycleaner.com/worksheets and Do You Have What it Takes questionnaire http://savvycleaner.com/do-you-have-what-it-takes
4. Set up your home office with computer and printer or go get a public library card and use theirs.
5. Go to the office supply store and pick up the office supplies you will need. Checklist of supplies http://savvycleaner.com/office-supplies

Day Two:

1. Order medical shoe covers and latex or nitrile gloves. (If you don't order them online, you may be able to pick up smaller amounts in the automotive department at Walmart that will tie you over until you have money coming in and can order a box online.

2. Print your ream of 500 pages = 1000 Flyers
3. Choose a territory (or neighborhoods) you will work in.
4. Answer questions from the Rules and Regulations section.

Day Three:

1. Run Flyers
2. Block out your schedule and the days and times you will be available to work. Be ready for the phone to start ringing and the slots to fill up.
3. Memorize answers from the Rules and Regulations section.
4. Print Worksheets and practice doing a walkthrough with family members at your own house. (This is your sales pitch and you want it to be as natural and fluid as possible.)

Day Four:

1. Memorize the red dialogue from the "how to bid a job" section word verbatim (it works.)
2. You will probably have calls coming in. Practice delivering the answers from the "Rules and Regulations" section to your prospective clients and tell them what forms of payment you accept.
3. Set cleaning appointments backed by a 100% satisfaction guarantee.

Day Five:

1. Go to Walmart and buy some basic cleaning supplies. We didn't have a chance to cover "how to clean" or what supplies you will need in this book. We have an extensive course on it in the "Fast Track to Success" course and you can tap into everything else you need to know about how to start your own house cleaning company and get credentials at SavvyCleaner.com http://www.savvycleaner.com/ but for now, click this link to download a Cleaning Supplies Shopping List to get you started for your business this week.

Day Six:

1. Clean your own house from top to bottom and see how long it takes you.
2. Clean your car from top to bottom – this is how your car will look from now on.

Day Seven:

1. This is your family day. Rejoice in them and celebrate the new life you are creating for them.
2. Rest up for next week – hopefully your calendar is now full from call-ins from your flyers.
3. Sign up for a weekly list of free Tips, Tricks and Time Saving Hacks for House Cleaners at http://savvycleaner.com/tips

This is not rocket science. There are no short cuts and no loopholes. Only a proven system that if followed exactly, applying the techniques you have learned here will put you on a path that will explode your house cleaning business. The future is ahead of you. Don't look back.

See you on the inside,

Angela
AngelaBrown@SavvyCleaner.com

BONUS:
PS. After this book went to press, I realized I left out a HUGE bonus - In the section on "Rules and Regulations" there are 63 questions that customers will ask you before they hire you. People hiring you will ask different questions depending on what is important to them. I've listed the questions but not the answers – The answers are different for everyone, and you will ultimately create your own answers. How I answer them is part of a paid training class we do over at www.SavvyCleaner.com and if you buy that training a-la-carte it is $129. Knowing how to answer those questions – and why I answer them the way I do will save you 8 years off the learning curve. So here is my deal: If you help me out with a review of this book, I will give you a voucher to attend that live training class at no charge. * The voucher is transferrable – so if you are not the person starting your own house cleaning company,

you may pass it along to a sibling, spouse, child, student, or friend looking for a job, niece, nephew or the person who currently cleans your house.

Here's how to get the voucher:

1) Login in your account on Amazon.
2) Click on this link http://amzn.to/1QVWUKN
3) Add this book to your wish list on Amazon and just leave it there (It helps my book rank higher in the search engines)
4) Follow the author (Hey that's me)
5) Give me a rating and a short review
6) Take a screen shot with your cell phone of your rating and review and email it to me at AngelaBrown@SavvyCleaner.com
7) Subject line of email: Book Review Complete – Please Send Bonus Voucher
8) Make sure you include your name and your email of where to send the voucher.

That is it! That is your good deed for the day and we both win.
THANK YOU IN ADVANCE FOR BEING SO AWESOME!

Made in the USA
Monee, IL
16 January 2023

25436298R00079